The Discursive Mind

The Discursive Mind

Rom Harré

Grant Gillett

SAGE Publications

International Educational and Professional Publisher

Thousand Oaks   London   New Delhi

For information address:

 SAGE Publications, Inc.
2455 Teller Road
Thousand Oaks, California 91320

SAGE Publications Ltd.
6 Bonhill Street
London EC2A 4PU
United Kingdom

SAGE Publications India Pvt. Ltd.
M-32 Market
Greater Kailash I
New Delhi 110 048 India

Printed in the United States of America

Library of Congress Cataloging-in-Publication Data

Harré, Rom.
    The discursive mind / Rom Harré, Grant Gillett.
      p. cm.
    Includes bibliographical references and index.
    ISBN 0-8039-5501-4. — ISBN 0-8039-5502-2 (pbk.)
    1. Discursive psychology.   I. Gillett, Grant, 1950-
II. Title.
BF201.3.H37   1994   93-43672
150—dc20

94 95 96 97 10 9 8 7 6 5 4 3 2 1

Sage Production Editor: Diane S. Foster

❖ Contents ❖

❖ Preface ❖

The rapid rise of "discursive psychology" in the last five years indicates the appearance of a genuinely "new psychology" compared with what has gone before. Behaviorism passed away, leaving only its experimental methodology behind, and even that is kept in being more by institutional pressures than by any scientific merit. The new dawn seemed to many to be heralded by the development of computer-oriented "cognitive science," but that too proved to be an illusion. The technical sophistication of the programming model was not matched by a coherent theory of the relation between formal computation and real-life human thought. Pressure from within cognitive psychology to achieve ecological validity led to an examination of human function in actual social and cultural settings. The ubiquitous role of symbol use in human life was immediately evident and has finally been reflected in an orientation in psychology that takes that fact centrally into account.

Discursive psychology is the culmination of a number of independent developments, reaching as far back as the work of G. H. Mead and L. Vygotsky. It incorporates such contemporary movements as ethnomethodology, social constructionism, and ethogenics. There has been a flood of new publications in the new style, but none of them is pitched at a level suitable for undergraduate study, nor do they attempt an overview of the new orientation and its working synthesis of linguistically oriented methods with the study of neuropsychology.

This book is an attempt to make the main tenets and some of the research results of discursive psychology easily available. It is meant too as an introduction to the forthcoming Sage text, the three-volume *Rethinking Psychology* edited by Rom Harré, Jonathan Smith, Luk van Langenhove, and Peter Stearns. Together the four volumes are intended to provide a basis for course work at both an intermediate and an advanced level.

Though the chapters in this book are new writing, the themes of several chapters have been developed in articles in *Common Knowledge, Theory and Psychology,* and *Research on Language and Social Interaction.*

In nearly every context in this book, psychological observations are meant to apply to human beings of either gender. To avoid some of the clumsy circumlocutions currently in use, we have adopted the vernacular device of the gender-neutral third person singular usage of *they, their,* and *them* as recommended by Muhlhausler and Harré (1991, Chap. 9).

We are grateful to Kevin Weinfurt, of the graduate psychology program at Georgetown University, for giving us a "student's eye" view of an earlier draft of this text, from which we drew some valuable lessons in more "user friendly" exposition.

❖ 1 ❖

A Clash of Paradigms

The Advent of Discursive Psychology

In this introductory book, we are going to try to cover those recent developments in psychology that have led to the movement that has come to be called discursive psychology. Our focus will be on psychology, but the influence of this movement is increasingly felt in all other branches of human studies. The movement we will be describing involves sociology, anthropology, and linguistics. The advent of discursive psychology has been in part the result of a synthesis of trends in these and other aspects of human science. Some of the material we shall be dealing with is easily seen as anthropology just as much as it is as psychology. Psychology, however, has changed much more than any other of the human sciences. Not only its transformation but its lack of transformation in the last 20 years have been quite extraordinary. It is both remarkable and interesting that the old psychologies continue to exist alongside the new ones. This is a phenomenon that should be of interest to sociologists of science. It is quite unique, so far as we know, in the history of science, that old, outdated, and manifestly inadequate ways of doing research, and untenable theories, have persisted alongside new and better theories and methods.

To understand where the new development has come from and its significance for human studies, we need to go back to have a look at the traditional, experimentalist psychology that still exists, particularly in the United States. On the side of method—how one does research—this psychology had its roots in behaviorism and its philosophical backing from the positivism of the 1920s. On the side of theory, it is cognitive, in the sense that it favors explanations in terms of mental states or processes. By drawing attention to some of its leading features, features that force us to reject this approach, we can build up our ideas of the new development by contrast.

The Psychology of the Tradition: The Old Paradigm and Its First Transformation

An Outline of Behaviorism and the Experimentalist Program

Psychology is the science that attempts to explain behavior. There are three components to this definition and each has been significant in the development of psychology in its contemporary form. We will need to consider all three to understand the nature of the cognitive revolutions to be discussed in this book. In the attempt to make psychology a science, many theorists were misled into thinking that the only permissible phenomena fitted to be material to be studied in a psychological *science* would be publicly observable entities. They mistakenly supposed that such were the phenomena of the paradigmatic physical sciences, inorganic chemistry and Newtonian mechanics. This led to the restriction of legitimate categories of phenomena to those that could be physically specified such as stimulus conditions, states of the environment detectable by the five senses (usually only vision was employed), and bodily movements as registered by some inhuman apparatus. What is more, both classes of phenomena were thought of as capable of being partitioned into independent or dependent variables. This suggested that there ought to be some simple and surveyable relationship between types of measurable events originating in the environment and equally measurable types of events originating in the organism and some, possibly complex but in principle discernible, set of laws that connected the two.

The idea of explanation in psychology was also assimilated to modes and models of explanation assumed (wrongly) to be in use in physical science apt to generate lawlike predictions linking simply specified antecedents and measurable outcomes. These linkages were often presented as causal relations, although in a truly positivist spirit all that usually was claimed was the existence of a statistical correlation between stimulus event types and response event types. There was a time in living and vivid memory when most of us worked under these restrictions in the project of trying to make sense of human beings. Of course, it was recognized at the outset that human beings might be too complex for this kind of investigation. Attention was focused on an ever-decreasing range of simpler organisms such as rats and pigeons (Beach, 1965). And even these animals were studied with complete disregard for their normal context of adaptation. The preoccupation was with mathematical laws linking simple patterns of stimulation to detectable overt movements, and anything that introduced complications (such as instinctive behaviors, physiological mechanisms influencing drive structure, response selection, or perceptual capabilities) was discarded as interfering with the scientific thrust of psychology. Ironically, at about the same time, the biology of animal behavior was undergoing a remarkable and permanent revolution at the hands of Lorenz, Tinbergen, and von Frisch, who abandoned the laboratory for the study of the whole lives of animals in their natural surroundings (McGill, 1965).

In the Old Paradigm, "behavior" was taken to be identical with detectable bodily movements and the patterns that showed up in strings of such movements. The idea that the movement or operation on the environment might have an ethological or cognitive context was taken as irrelevant in the face of its role as a response to some antecedent event controlled by the investigator. "Good" subjects for research were those whose operations—"responses"—could be found that would show lawlike regularities in their relations to a fairly narrow range of definable antecedent conditions.

The Metaphysical Roots of the Old Paradigm

Traditional, experimental psychology—the Old Paradigm, as we have sketched it—was based not only on an outdated philosophical theory of science but also on a much criticized metaphysical thesis regarding human beings. It assumed mind-body dualism, sometimes called Cartesianism after René Descartes, the most famous exponent of the idea that human beings are composed of two systems, one mental and one material, realized in two distinct and very different substances. The body with its chemical, pneumatic, mechanical, and electrical mechanisms was made of physical stuff; the mind with its thoughts, feelings, recollections, and images was made of mental stuff. Although the idea that there were two distinct kinds of "stuff" quickly lost its appeal, the idea that the mental life was "inner," as distinct from behavior, which was "outer," lingered on. Thus there were mental processes going on in the mind stuff, but they could not become part of the subject matter of a psychological science, according to the adherents of the Old Paradigm, because they were inaccessible to public scrutiny. Hypotheses about them were immune from public testing. The behaviorists, with the possible exception of J. B. Watson, mostly believed in the existence of some sort of mental realm. For example, B. F. Skinner argued that at least some classes of "mental phenomena" were to be classified among human behavior and studied in the same manner as other classes of behaviors. Whether this had any cash value in the light of the experimental paradigm that Skinner adopted is a moot point. Despite Clark Hull's hypothetico-deductive program, the experimental method, as we have described it in our account of the Old Paradigm, developed in such a way as to involve no reference to mental processes at all.

Some Drawbacks of
Old Paradigm Psychology

Some very important problems of this way of trying to set up a scientific psychology were soon noticed. Whatever Old Paradigm psychology was, it was not anything like a *science* in the accepted sense of that rather eclectic term. It was realized that the interpretation of experimental manipulations, as recorded in the writings of psychologists, depended upon their ideas about what was happening in the laboratory and what they were manipulating when they subjected people to their controlled patterns of stimuli. The people who took part in the experiments were not asked what they thought was happening because they were studied in the way that one would study objects. Indeed, in the heyday of experimentalism, an essential part of the methodology was the systematic deception of the "subjects." The experimental manipulations were interpreted by the experimenters in terms of their own concepts, and the responses of the participants in the "experiments" were also interpreted in terms of the very same concepts.

Which concepts were they? They were the concepts of common sense, though almost always dressed up in impressive but imprecise neologisms. But common sense takes a variety of forms! Which commonsense concepts were drawn upon? Well, they were the commonsense concepts of middle-class American academics. When one looked at the descriptions of experiments about remembering, about emotions, about attitudes, about personalities, with an eye to the basic conceptual structures in terms of which they had been set up and later interpreted, they all involved concepts that had come from a particular culture, with a particular set of moral, political, and psychological assumptions.

It is not surprising that anthropologists have played a large part in the development of alternative foundations for psychology, given that they are professionally aware, so to speak, of the diversity of commonsense systems with which subtle and psychologically sophisticated ways of life are managed. Mainstream psychologists, with their narrow training and cultural isolation, have not generally been aware of how local their commonsense systems are.

Equally important was the realization that the program depended on a particular and generally rejected philosophical theory of causality. When one looks at the way the results of this kind of work were presented, one sees a mere array of correlations. What sort of philosophical framework did the statistical presentation of these correlations as laws of behavior fit into? It became very clear that it belonged to the Humean tradition; that is, causation is nothing but a regular pattern among sequences of events. The laws of nature are simply catalogues of correlations of phenomena.

The First Steps
Toward a Cognitive Science

The major crack in this tight circle of frenzied and stereotyped investigative activity was best shown by a joke.

> *Rat:* Boy have I got this guy well trained, every time I press the bar he gives me food.

The joke highlights the importance of what goes on in the "black box" connecting input to output. And even if we regard the joke as highly inaccurate in its implications about the cognition of such animals as rats, it is highly accurate about, indeed modeled on, the behavior of human beings. In human behavior, it is vitally important to understand not only the external conditions but how those conditions are interpreted and understood by the subject.

No one suggests that the subject matter which the physicist, the chemist, the botanist, or geologist seeks to order and make sensible, at the same time may seek to order and make sense of him. This, however, is perhaps the single most outstanding feature of the field of events which the psychologist has chosen to study—people. (Bannister and Mair, 1968, p. 3)

This contention is supported by a psychophysiology experiment in which human subjects were trained on an expectancy task. This task links a warning stimulus to an imperative stimulus in such a way that subjects produce an electrical wave in their frontal lobes—called a readiness potential—at the appropriate time before they are required to respond. But when subjects are told that there will no longer be an imperative stimulus to respond, they stop producing the readiness potential. Thus the subject's understanding of the situation rather than mere stimulus pairings is important in what is going on neurologically as a result of the warning stimulus (Walter, 1968).

The Sources of the Impetus for Change

The "New" Social Psychology

Change came from two directions. First of all, there was a new paradigm proposed for social psychology. According to the "ethogenic" point of view, people were to be taken to be active beings, using rules and other normative constraints in jointly constructing their social relations and the episodes in which they were realized in action. The term *ethogenics* was coined on the analogy of "ethology," the new science of animal behavior that had been developed by the study of animal life in its real environments. Ethogenics was to be the study of the genesis of meaningful conduct or accountable behavior. A number of important empirical studies were carried out using the methods proposed by adherents to the ethogenic point of view.

Some of the key ideas of the ethogenic point of view in social psychology had been anticipated long since in the symbolic interactionist approach to human studies, which took its start from the work of G. H. Mead (1934). The idea of the social world as a discursive construction, with all the implications that idea might have for social psychology, was quite well developed in the nineteen seventies, particularly in the work of Lyman and Scott (1970). These authors were also responsible for one of the early attempts to explore the dramaturgical model of life as theater (and theater as life) in the studies of Shakespearean anticipations of the symbolic interactionist point of view (Lyman and Scott, 1975).

The "New" Cognitive Psychology

But of greater importance on the larger scene than the developments in social psychology were the beginnings of cognitive psychology at Harvard, about the same time, initiated by J. S. Bruner (1973) and G. A. Miller and P. N. Johnson-Laird (1976). They began a movement that, with hindsight, we can see as the first cognitive revolution. This involved the introduction of a way of thinking about human beings that rejected the whole framework of method and metaphysics upon which the experimentalist tradition had been based. To understand the advent of discursive psychology as a second cognitive revolution, the final apotheosis of the New Paradigm, we have to look at the first cognitive revolution, its successes and its ultimate failure to push the transformation of psychology right through.

Bruner and Miller proposed the return to some very fundamental conceptions of the psychology of human beings, which were to be found in the most elementary of basic Cartesian ideas. The architects of the first cognitive revolution were mentalists, in the sense that they took for granted that there were mental processes "behind" what people could be observed to do. They thought, however, that the way that this had been interpreted in the experimental, behaviorist tradition—namely, as a reason for ignoring the mind—was seriously mistaken. What was wrong was the prohibi-

tion on the study of cognitive processes and states. Both the behaviorists and their successors, the new cognitivists, thought that
these mental processes were inaccessible to public observation. It
is very important to understand that behaviorists and cognitivists
shared the Cartesian metaphysics of mind. But they were worlds
apart as to the significance of this fact for the design of a science
of psychology.

The idea that made the program of a new cognitive science seem
possible was the importation of a different conception of scientific
work. The new conception can be traced to two sources: a clearer
view of the nature of physical science and the advent of the first
stirrings of postpositivist philosophy of science. It is not clear from
Bruner's autobiography, nor from George Miller's writings, whether
either had these sources consciously in mind during the period of
their collaboration.

The Hypothetico-Deductive Account
of Scientific Explanation

From Descartes in the seventeenth century to Hempel in the
twentieth, philosophers have tried to give an account of scientific
explanation that used only logical concepts. Science was supposed
to identify the basic elements of the world and then explain all
their combinations and properties by a set of logical or mathematical calculations. For instance, one could identify a gene by noting
the mathematical patterns of inheritance in a certain group of organisms and then positing that these arose from a package of genetic
material with certain properties in relation to other packages. Call
the gene $g1$ and then say that we posit other relevant genes $g2$ and
$g3$. Let us say that we derive the following hypotheses:

$g1$ and $g2$ lead to a brain tumor
$g1$ and $g2$ and $g3$ do not lead to a brain tumor

We test these and find that they are confirmed and formulate a
theory, based on the logical and observed relationships that $g3$ is

a suppressor gene for a tumor-producing process caused by $g1$ and $g2$ in combination. When we discern further features associated with $g1$ and $g2$ and $g3$, we would construct a little more theory until we had a fairly complex way of thinking about the genetic causes of cancer based on observations of and deductions from patterns of inheritance.

The aim was to try to extract a common logical form from all kinds of scientific explanations. Some domain of phenomena, D, contains items of types a, b, and c, and under conditions x, y, and z, interactions occur in accordance with laws L_1, L_2, and L_3. According to this point of view, an explanation and hence a theory consisting of a group of hypotheses, from which, with the addition of some definitions and descriptions of the conditions under which an experimental test or observation was conducted, one drew a sentence expressing possible laws as logical consequences. Then one tried to see whether the statements one had deduced were correct or incorrect. If one's deduction referred to a future event, it was a prediction; if to an event already known, the hypotheses and so on from which it had been deduced counted as an explanation of the event in question (Hempel, 1965). On the basis of the success or failure of these predictions and explanations, one assessed the scientific value of the hypotheses.

Systems of hypotheses could be tested indirectly (as in our genetics example). If they could be taken to describe unobservable entities, processes, and structures, in the mind, they played the role of genuine psychological theories. In the context of the structure of the deductive-nomological model of explanatory theories, theorizing in psychology could, once again, be taken seriously. The problem of the inaccessibility of the mind for a science of psychology was overcome, in just the same way that the inaccessibility of electrons for a science of electricity (or genes for a theory of heredity) had been overcome by physicists (or biologists). The hypothetico-deductive method alone was not the key. A theory in psychology had a characteristic structure: There would be a set of hypotheses concerning unobservable cognitive processes that were to be tested by examining their deductive consequences. It did not matter whether the hypotheses were about accessible or inaccessible states and processes. They would all be subject to public testing via their consequences. Thus, for instance, we might posit a single channel processing mechanism for encoding and decoding memory traces and deduce that different packages of remembered information might interfere with one another if the subject attempted to do cognitive tasks using old information while remembering new information. If we found this effect, it would be said to support the hypothesis (although there are, in fact, quite a number of different interpretations available). By doing other related experiments, we might narrow the viable hypotheses down until one emerged as a favored candidate for a model of human memory. Whether the model could stand depended not on its logical powers but on its ontological plausibility. The fact that some hypothetico-deductive structure could be erected had been known, since the sixteenth century, to be scientifically inconclusive. In the absence of a strong criterion of ontological plausibility, that is, a specification of what sorts of things hypothetical states and processes could be, an infinity of hypotheses of equal logical power could, in principle, be constructed.

Bruner and Miller, though they would perhaps not be happy to be so labeled, were, in a very general sense, not only hypothetico-deductivists but also Cartesians. They believed in the existence of inner mental states and processes. By using the framework of the hypothetico-deductive conception of theory, they thought that one could create a human science that got over the difficulty that had spawned the unsatisfactory metaphysics of behaviorism. They called their new approach "cognitive science."

It is worth noticing that Freudian psychology, as customarily interpreted, has exactly the same logical structure as the new "cognitive science" had. The Freudians assumed that the important things about human cognition were not accessible even to the person in whom they were happening. The Freudian unconscious was very like the cognitive psychologists' "inaccessible mind," unobservable but active. Fundamental cognitive processes were supposed to be occurring in the unconscious. According to the Freudians, these hidden processes and structures were influential, even fateful, in people's lives. How could one test whether hypotheses concerning repressed contents and unconscious complexes were true? One tried to find observable logical consequences of hypotheses about the complexes that had been created by repression, for instance, in their effects in the symbolism of dreams, in the symptoms of neurotic behavior, in slips of the tongue, and so on. In just the same way as the cognitive scientist, so Freudian psychologists could test hypotheses about their favorite inaccessible cognitive structures by the hypothetico-deductive method. The difference between Bruner and Miller on the one hand and Freudians on the other was not a difference of philosophical viewpoint underlying the method. There were, however, major differences in the rigor of the methods used and also in what they thought there was in the mind.

There is a second general feature of the hypothetico-deductive point of view that has been of great historical importance. We expect the tests of a scientific hypothesis to be publicly replicable, and we also expect the results to be universally applicable. Bruner and Miller and all those who followed after them assumed that the mental system, the mental machinery revealed by the use of the hypothetico-deductive method, was, at a rather low level of abstraction, the same in all human beings. We shall follow Shweder (1992) in calling this the hypothesis of the central processing mechanism, the "CPM." Accordingly, the differences that anthropologists and linguists discover in the cognitive performances and techniques of culturally and historically remote peoples are superficial.

The Metaphysics of the Cognitive Science Program

When this conception of science as the indirect testing of theory was examined carefully by philosophers of science, however, something very striking emerged. One notices that the hypotheses at the core of any theory are not freely constructed. There are very strong constraints on the hypotheses one can entertain. If one is trying to think up a hypothesis to explain electrical phenomena, one makes up hypotheses about the behavior of electrons. One doesn't use psychological concepts, like love and hate, for instance. Why not? Such concepts would not be in keeping with our general picture of the world. That picture does not come from observation: It is part of our *meta*-physics. When cognitive scientists started making up hypotheses about human cognition, they used concepts like "concept," "logical operation," "processing of information," and so on. Why those? They are the concepts of mentation, and if we believe that there is a hidden mental world, our *meta*-psychology would enjoin us to use just these concepts.

Philosophers call the totality of such assumptions the "ontology" of the science, because it is a kind of list of the things we believe that the world in question is actually made up of. To understand how any particular theory is created, why the hypotheses are the way they are, we must look into the ontological assumptions that constrain the formulation of those hypotheses.

As cognitive science developed, these constraints became sharper and more specific. The basic idea of a mental mechanism persisted. But what ontological constraints determine, in detail, how we are going to determine in more detail the sort of hypothetical mental mechanisms we permit ourselves to imagine? In the original version of cognitive science, the basis of Bruner and Miller's first cognitive revolution, there was one particular and very widespread idea, that of rule-following. A process analogous to the everyday process of following rules would produce uniform and orderly forms of behavior just as an assembly line would produce cars. And this idea of rule-following was itself based on ways in which natural mechanisms obey laws of nature. Rules were inserted into the hidden recesses of the mind. They appeared in different guises. There were the scripts of Schank and Abelson (1977); there were grammars of the linguists influenced by Chomsky (1972); there was the role-rule model of Harré and Secord (1973); and many others. All these theoreticians thought that the mental mechanisms, hypotheses about which would be the basis of theories in the new cognitive science, were essentially versions of rule-following. There must be rules in the mind and somehow they are followed, and it is this that is responsible for orderly behavior. This idea received its fullest development in the famous book by Miller, Galanter, and Pribram (1967), *Plans and the Structure of Behavior.* The CPM, the central processing mechanism, was a device for performing nonconscious rule-following.

Computation as the Prime Model for Mental Activity

It was not long before another model, not another ontology but an influential supplement to it, began to appear on the scene. The problem that was left over after the adoption of the rule-following model was how such processes were actually implemented. The brain must be the device that is implementing the rules. Brains are the hardware. The moment one starts to talk this way, one has entered the path to the artificial intelligence version of the first cognitive revolution.

The next step was to give a further analysis of the hypothetical mental activity, to treat it as like the running of a program. The brain or its modules are processing information just as computers are. "Running a program" not only would be the most technically sophisticated expression of the idea of rule-following, a convenient and powerful metaphor, but it also could be the basis of a methodology. According to the "Turing Test," it should be possible to write a program that, when run on a computer, yields output that, suitably interpreted, would be indistinguishable from the behavior of a human being in similar circumstances. In the conception of the information processing model, it seemed that psychology had now found a format that would allow it to become fully scientific, in the realist sense. Its theories would consist of hypotheses about information processing mechanisms. Predictions, describing behavior, could be drawn from these hypotheses. All forms of activity including the use of speech, the display of emotions, the evincing of attitudes, the solving of problems, and so on ought to be comprehendible in principle.

In this way the naturalistic rule-following model developed into the highly nonnaturalistic "program" of artificial intelligence, as the most systematic way of developing the conception of rules in the light of the computational analogy. The brain is to the computer as mental activity is to the running of the program. To do psychology, one tries to write programs that, when run on a computer, will simulate what people do in trying to carry out this or that project in particular circumstances.

The first cognitive revolution ushered back onto the stage the study of cognitive processes in psychology. Cognitive psychologists attempted to understand the mechanisms that mediated the transition from stimulus to response by examining such things as semantic categorization and its effect on recall of information, explicit instructions and problem-solving strategies, the effect of cognitive anticipations on perception, the relationship between images and propositions in the internal processes subserving cognition, the hierarchical relationships between categories in the ordering and retrieval of knowledge. The overall model was that the mind was an internal realm of operations and computations hypotheses that could be tested by experimental tests of their logical consequences via the systematic manipulation of specifiable inputs and outputs to the black box of cognition.

In developmental psychology, there was a focus on the kinds of operations that could be performed by the developing cognitive subject and on what kinds of structures must underpin these. The idea evolved of a hierarchy of operations in which logico-mathematically formed structures of thought gradually assembled a cognitive specification of the world from the evidence or data presented to the individual. Even in personality theory, there was a move away from the positing of unconscious mechanisms and traits that, for Freudians, determined behavior, to a focus on the cognitive world of the subject and the way in which he or she constructed "reality as experienced" (Kelly, 1955). This focus on the cognitive attributes of the subject was, however, still motivated primarily by an interest in a world that could be objectified according to the traditional metaphysics of "Newtonian common sense." It did not need to regard the ways the subjects took themselves to be conceptualizing the world as more than phenomena to be explored and studied by the experimenter.

The philosopher par excellence of this move in psychology was Immanuel Kant. He went beyond Hume and the early empiricists to emphasize the need to take seriously the rational structure of the mind and the way that the mind synthesized or ordered experience on the basis of its cognitive capacities. Kant discussed the rules of the understanding as psychologists might discuss cognitive mechanisms. He saw these rules as working on sensory material to generate internal representations of the world that were accurate or objectively valid when the individual obeyed the rational principles governing thought and knowledge. It was, however, a different strand of philosophy that led some psychologists to attempt the reorientation of psychology.

Conclusion

Experimental psychology grew out of the behaviorist program. That program was based on a philosophical theory about the nature of the mind. The mind was taken to be a private arena not available as a source of data for a science of human action. Only the statistical relations between external stimuli and overt responses could be the subject matter of a psychological science. These relations could be discovered, it was thought, by the manipulation of the values of independent variables, representing stimuli, on the lookout for correlated changes in the values of dependent variables. The experimental methodology survived the demise of behaviorist theory. It has come to be called the Old Paradigm. The drawbacks of this approach to psychology were soon seen to far outweigh any advantages it might have had.

Cognitive psychology was based on a revival of the use of mentalistic concepts in psychological theorizing. Experiments survived as tests of the behavioral consequences of hypotheses about the performances of supposed information processing "mechanisms." These hypotheses were developed through the exploitation of the analogy between computers and human brains. The notion of a "rule" began to play a large part in psychological theorizing, serving as ultimate explanatory concept. It seemed as if, at last, psychology had some claim to be one among the sciences. But, alas, as we shall see, this optimism was premature.

❖ 2 ❖

The Second Cognitive Revolution

Meaning Versus Representation

The new and different strand of psychology was found, most influentially, in the later writings of Wittgenstein (1953). He argued that we understand the behavior of an individual when we grasp the meanings that are informing that person's activity. His early philosophy was entirely congenial with the understanding of the mind as a Cartesian realm in which subjects built up a picture of the world from their contact with it. The mind, so conceived, had direct relations to primitive features of reality, read off pictures of structured combinations of those features from states of affairs in the actual world, and performed logical operations on the resulting (pictured) combinations of those features. In his later philosophy, he rejected this picture theory almost in its entirety. Because this picture theory is a philosophical analogue of the theory of representation as used in certain strands of current psychology, it is well worth taking note of the reasons for Wittgenstein's rejection of it and the understanding of persons and their thoughts that he erected in its place.

Wittgenstein came to see that he had failed to elucidate the nature of understanding. The picture (*bild*) of the world was of no more use than the state of affairs itself in trying to capture the semantic or representational relation—what it is for something to mean something. The picture was an inert inner structure and the real work of comprehending what it was to understand and use such a picture—that is, to think or cognize—had not been started. What use is it to have a picture in your head? All that means is that you have close-up or inner version of the problem with which you started. As he struggled with this realization, he came gradually to see that understanding and the phenomena of meaning or intentionality in general could only be approached by looking at what people actually do with word patterns and other sign systems. He formulated the doctrine that meaning is the use to which we put our signs. He studied the use of words in "language games," by which he meant complex activities involving both the use of language and the use of physical tools and actions, where they were ordinarily encountered.

He came to see that mental activity is not essentially a Cartesian or inner set of processes but a range of moves or techniques defined against a background of human activity and governed by informal rules. These rules, unlike the rules-laws at work in supposed inner, cognitive processes, were the rules that people actually followed. They are most evident when we consider the correct and incorrect ways of using words. We can then broaden our vision beyond that to appreciate that there are right and wrong ways of using all concepts. For instance, one cannot (should not!) think of a sheep as a carnivorous mammal, of a red object as being blue, or of a square as being round, because those thoughts would violate the rules of correct usage. "Sheep are carnivorous" is not false, but senseless. The rules governing the use of signs (concept use) permeate and structure the intentional or mental lives of human beings. They are discernible and explicable when we locate them in the language games and forms of life where the people who follow them live their lives. In the absence of an appreciation of the working of the relevant rule-governed tracts of human activity, we cannot understand the meanings that inform the behavior of a human being.

Imagine that we had accepted this lesson about human behavior in general. We would still not forget the rules in play in human activity because, if we wish to discern the meaning of a particular behavior or appreciate the goal of some performance, we would need to know which rules the individual was following at that point. Thus we would need to know where and how the individual locates his or her current behavior in relation to the context that obtains then and there. In this sense, the psychological is not reducible to or replaceable by explanations in terms of physiology, physics, or any other point of view that does not reveal the structure of meanings existing in the lives of the human group to which the subject of an investigation belongs.

This understanding of human activity requires us to interpret the behavior of another according to some appreciation of the self-positioning of the subject within the complex structure of rules and practices within which that individual moves (Winch, 1958). To latch on to this structure and how it informs the activity of an individual—say, Manaio—it is not sufficient to observe Manaio as a complex mechanism geared to respond in certain ways. We have to get inside the forms of life and the norms, conventions, rules, and so on in which Manaio's activities have taken shape. This requires the kind of understanding Weber called *verstehen*. It is based on an empathic identification with the other that helps the observer make sense of what the other is doing. Such an approach to the understanding of behavior can be sensitive to the subtleties of the situation of the other in a way that an attempt to identify and isolate a surveyable number of objective independent variables cannot be. We would say that we need to know what a situation means to a person and not just what the situation is (say, according to a description in terms of its physical characteristics as these are seen by an observer) if we are to understand what that person is doing. Imagine, for example, the markings on a bush trail that a European tourist might ignore but that instantly would be read by an Aboriginal tracker and would guide him immediately to his quarry. Here the marks are, in a certain sense, the same for each observer—a bent twig, a crushed flower—but their meaning differs according to their place in the current perspective of each traveler.

Once one sees the task of understanding human behavior as involving interpretation and empathy rather than prediction or control, the self-reports of the people one is studying become very important in any psychological research project. And these should not be taken as (falsifiable) reports of states of mind but as expressions of how things are to the subject. Thus the experimenter or observer has to enter into a discourse with the people being studied and try to appreciate the shape of the subject's cognitive world. But at this point it no longer makes sense to talk of observers and subjects at all. There are only coparticipants in the project of making sense of the world and our experience of it.

The Central Place of Discourse

It is a small step from here to the inclusion of a second aspect of Wittgenstein's later philosophy and to a further conceptual revolution in our understanding of psychology. Concepts, the basis of thinking, are expressed by words, and words are located in languages, which are used to accomplish a huge variety of tasks. By using words and significant gestures, we reprimand wrongdoers, we issue invitations, we give interpersonal (purportedly) factual reports, we engage in intrapersonal reflections on our plans for the future, show that a person is not an isolated cognizer or interpreter of the world but is engaged with others in practical, ceremonial, and communicative activities, constituting forms of life in which language is taught and learned (Quinton, 1967). Thus the discourses constructed jointly by persons and within sociocultural groups become an important part of the framework of interpretation. If the mind is to be understood as a domain of skills and techniques that renders the world meaningful to the individual, then our conception of the mind as a Cartesian entity sealed into its own individual and self-contained subjectivity must be revised. We must learn to see the mind as the meeting point of a wide range of structuring influences whose nature can only be painted on a broader canvas than that provided by the study of individual organisms.

In this view, our delineation of the subject matter of psychology has to take account of discourses, significations, subjectivities, and positionings, for it is in these that psychological phenomena *actually* exist. For example, an attitude should not be seen as a semipermanent mental entity, causing people to say and do certain things. Rather, it comes into existence in displays expressive of decisions and judgments and in the performance of actions. (We shall argue in Chapter 9 that emotions are also to be thought of in this way.) Each reconceptualization helps to draw our attention to the fact that the study of the mind is a way of understanding the phenomena that arise when different sociocultural discourses are integrated within an identifiable human individual situated in relation to those discourses.

For many who have not grasped the full import of the discursive turn, this drift in the theoretical base of psychology threatens to destroy its subject matter entirely. It seems to make the mind of an individual person into a mere nexus or meeting point of social relations. In this reading, it seems as if the mind lacks any independent reality as a self-existent cluster of processes and states.

The idea that the mind is, in some sense, a social construction is true in that our concepts arise from our discourse and shape the way we think. This goes for the concepts that concern what is around us and also for the concepts that concern our own mental lives. Therefore the way in which we conceptualize the mind (or anything else) is a product of the concepts available within our discourse. When I think of love as a passion or an emotion that overtakes a person when exposed to the sight of another person, I will tend to describe my own and others' behavior in these terms (which would include "love at first sight"!) rather than, say, describing the love between two people as a joint creation deliberately fashioned over time and built on shared experience. The example of love is one that is particularly apt to illustrate the shift in the fundamentals of psychology that is contemplated. If one considers love to be a universal and unitary phenomenon that can come upon any and every human being at any point in his or her life, then, as a psychologist of the emotions, one should try to identify just that experience that should be represented as the state of "being in love." The questions one asks will be of the type: "Has it really happened yet?" "Is this how I should represent myself as being if I am really in love?" and so on. Now notice the dual assumptions: that there is a phenomenon here to be recognized, and that there is a definite way in which it should be represented. This poses only one form of question to the participant in a psychological investigation. That question-form takes as given states of affairs and forms of representation as essentially independent components in the act of knowing. But we might also ask what significance is to be given to a set of discourse-related events by the persons involved in them. If that significance involves the concept <love>, then their subjective experiences and perceived location in that discourse will change. As a lover, one occupies a certain place in relation to the social and moral order, one's acts and feelings take on meanings that they would otherwise not have. And these meanings carry further entailments in terms of reactions, actions, feelings, and expectations related to the positionings with which they are associated. Thus, in reconceptualizing these events according to discursive psychology, one would notice the dynamic interplay between the meanings invoked in understanding a situation and the psychological character of that situation. This calls in question the simple idea that there is a situation and a quite separate representation of the situation. Therefore we use the term *signification* to indicate the active role of meaning in structuring the interaction between a person and a context so as to define the subjectivity of that person in the situation and their positioning in relation to certain discourses implicit in that subjectivity.

We have now encountered the idea that events and objects are given significance by the discourses in which they appear and that these significations both arise from and in part constitute the subjectivity of an individual in relation to what is signified. This may seem to suggest that there is no truth about the mind or the content of psychology, which, on the revised account, seems radically subject to different constructions. But things are not so unbound as they may seem.

Anyone has to negotiate his or her life events in such a way as to reconcile three distinct sets of constraints.

1. The need to adapt to situations that are, in some respects, independent of one's will (as Wittgenstein puts it) means that there is not infinite flexibility in the way one conceptualizes a situation. If I find myself in a room with only one door, then my ability to escape from that room is dependent upon my ability to recognize some part of my context as being a door, and in my actually so recognizing it. Absent this cognitive move, my activity will be severely limited.

2. The ways of conceptualizing things that come into play in a given occasion are required to cohere, to "hang together," to some extent. If they do not, I may have conflicting, confusing, or inconclusive orientations toward the situation in which I find myself. This drive for consistency can be overstated and the constraints it imposes are negotiable (to say the least) but they are nevertheless real. Thus, if I think of this person as seeking to oppress and exploit me, it will be hard also to think of them as enabling me to express and fulfill my own plans and projects. Seeing the situation under both aspects will require some adjustment so that one or the other wins out and I assimilate my subjective orientation and my consequent significations to one type of discourse or the other. Of course, as Billig (1988) has amply demonstrated, the social psychology of some common forms of life is radically contradictory.

For example, in his study of the survivors of heart attacks, he showed that these people are required simultaneously to be both well and ill. At a less "political" level, if I think of a certain tree as lying to the north of me then I cannot simultaneously think of it as lying to the south of me. Trees are not like that. This combination of thoughts are incompatible in such a way that they do not allow me to undertake any actions in relation to the tree.

3. I inhabit many different discourses each of which has its own cluster of significations. Some of these, as we have already noted, will conflict with one another and require negotiation and adjustment to be cotenable. This balancing, integrating, or correcting feature of mental life means that a particular type of discourse is unlikely to hold unbounded sway over the subjectivity of an individual. Indeed, when it does, we tend to think of that person as obsessed or fanatical. In any event, most of us will fashion a complex subjectivity from participation in many different discourses that tend mutually to illuminate one another to some extent and therefore to constrain the significations we apply to a given situation.

This last point has served somewhat to answer the question about the reality of the mind. In the present view, it is obvious that an individual person in discourse with others is a meeting point of many discourses and must, to some extent, integrate the multifaceted subjectivity that arises from this intersection of influences. We will therefore identify a person as having a coherent mind or personality to the extent that individuals can be credited with adopting various positions within different discourses and fashioning for themselves, however intentionally or unintentionally, a unique complex of subjectivities (essentially private discourses) with some longitudinal integrity. In this sense, there is a psychological reality to each individual. The difference between the mind or personality as seen in this way and the traditional view is that we see it as dynamic and essentially embedded in historical, political, cultural, social, and interpersonal contexts. It is not definable in isolation. And to be a psychological being at all, one must be in possession of some minimal repertoire of the cluster of skills necessary to the management of the discourses into which one may from time to time enter.

This, in brief, is the rationale and agenda of discursive psychology. It aims to take seriously the discursive subject as one of us. The subject is discursive in that he or she uses symbols whose meaning is a function of their use in discourse. Discourse involves both symbolic interactions and the conventions and relationships in which those interactions are constrained by informal rules and interconnected with each other in ways that reflect "the order of things," as Foucault called it. People are constantly operating in the midst of evaluative and interpersonal influences that shape and direct their activity. People are also agents who have their own construals and expressive acts to produce from the contexts in which they are embedded and within which we all live and move and have our being. For this reason, we cannot fully specify the psychological subject/agent as an object whose nature can be defined in isolation from a context and whose mental processes can be unraveled by objective measurement and description. As persons among us, our "subjects" relate to us and construe us even as we relate to and construe them. We all share and negotiate conceptualizations and significations according to the discourses in which we are adept. Psychological investigation cannot lose sight of these realities.

In what follows, we will try to show how the resulting philosophical reconstruction of psychology goes about conceptualizing the subject matter of the science of human behavior. This is the second cognitive revolution, the final shift of paradigms.

The Main Principles of the Second Cognitive Revolution

Let us sum up the discussion so far in terms of three leading principles that characterize the new cognitive psychology, that represent the discursive turn.

1. Many psychological phenomena are to be interpreted as properties or features of discourse, and that discourse might be public or private. As public, it is behavior; as private, it is thought.
2. Individual and private uses of symbolic systems, which in this view constitute thinking, are derived from interpersonal discursive processes that are the main feature of the human environment.
3. The production of psychological phenomena, such as emotions, decisions, attitudes, personality displays, and so on, in discourse depends upon the skill of the actors, their relative moral standing in the community, and the story lines that unfold.

These principles have certain implications, one being that discursive phenomena, for example, acts of remembering, are not manifestations of hidden subjective, psychological phenomena. They *are* the psychological phenomena. Sometimes they have subjective counterparts; sometimes they do not. There is no necessary shadow world of mental activity behind discourse in which one is working things out in private. This viewpoint amounts to a fundamental denial of the Cartesian view of human beings, not least because it denies that the workings of the mind are inaccessible. The workings of each other's minds are available to us in what we jointly create conversationally, and if our private mental activity is also symbolic, using essentially the same system, then we can make it available or not, as the situation seems to require it.

The Idea of Discourse

Another important consequence of the second cognitive revolution is the priority that must be given to ordinary languages in defining what are the phenomena for a scientific psychology. We will endeavor as far as possible to present and understand cognition in terms of the ordinary languages through which we think, rather than looking for abstract representations of them. That is radical because it resists the idea that a new, formal calculus must be devised to represent thought. Such calculi lie at the heart of the artificial intelligence project, the methodological principles of Chomsky and the transformational grammarians, and the assumption of formalists of all kinds.

We want now to develop the idea of discourse and the idea of an ontology for that central idea. Here are two brief passages on the idea of discourse from Potter and Edwards (1992, p. 2). First:

> The focus of discursive psychology is the action orientation of talking and writing [that is, what talk and writing is being used to do].

The second is this:

> Rather than seeing such discursive constructions as expressions of the speaker's underlying cognitive states, they are examined in the context of their occurrence as situated and occasioned constructions whose precise nature makes sense to participants and analysts alike in terms of the social action these descriptions accomplish.

That rather elaborate remark is a way of introducing the idea of the speech-act, this great Austinian idea that language in use is primarily concerned with the performance of actions and acts of various kinds.

Actions and the acts they accomplish make up discursive practices, an idea of which we will be making considerable use. A discursive practice is the repeated and orderly use of some sign system, where these uses are intentional, that is, directed at or to something. Much of the time we use intentional signs without consciously intending them for this or that or the other purpose. Discursive activities are always subject to standards of correctness and incorrectness. These standards can be expressed in terms of rules. Therefore a discursive practice is the use of a sign system, for which there are norms of right and wrong use, and the signs concern or are directed at various things.

The use of the word *I* in English is a discursive practice. One of its many roles is in the act of taking responsibility by a speaker for what he or she says and to what he or she is committed by the saying of it. According to the discursive point of view, in this and similar discursive practices of reflexive talk, I constitute myself as a self, as an embodied moral unit in the world. By using the indexical word *I,* I create my moral individuality for you or for anyone else whom I might address. I may even use it to address myself. The discursive practice of using the first person pronoun, or (in a language that does not have them or does not use them very much), using a first person inflection puts myself at the center of the activity and the way I use it affects its content and the attributions arising from it. Thus *espero* in Spanish means "I am waiting." Putting *yo* in front of *espero* makes my speech-act very emphatic, perhaps it could even be heard as a reprimand.

An Ontology for Discursive Psychology

We must now bring out the basic ontology of our world of psychology according to the discursive viewpoint. In reading the next section, it will be helpful to consult the chart below (Table 2.1). An ontology is a systematic exposition of the assumptions about the basic categories of beings admitted to the universe assumed in some scientific field.

TABLE 2.1 Two Ontologies

Ontologies	Locative Systems	Entities	Relations
Newtonian	Space and time	Things and events	Causality
Discursive	Arrays of people	Speech acts	Rules and story lines

The first step in setting out an ontology is to define the location system by which things and events in our "world" are to be individuated. We are going to need some way of saying where things are in the world we are going to describe. Let us compare what we shall call a "Newtonian" ontology, expressing the mechanical world picture, with a "Vygotskian" ontology for psychology.

In the Newtonian ontology, we have a system of locations in the manifolds of places (Space) and of moments (Time). We use that system to individuate the thinglike entities of the Newtonian universe. Something that occupies a place and a time is a different being than something that occupies a different place at the same time, even if they have all their properties in common. We have a location system that enables us to answer the questions: Where is it? Which is it? And when is it? An ontology for discursive psychology will therefore need its appropriate locative system for its basic entities.

We also need some conception of what the basic entities are in the Newtonian system. They are things and events. This is not something we discover but a decision we make about which aspects of our complex world are to occupy our attention as scientists. Discursive psychology will need to specify its basic entities too.

Finally, our ontology needs to specify a basic system of relations, which binds together the basic entities to create a world. In the Newtonian scheme, there are various kinds of causality that link things and events together.

We will use this brief sketch of the Newtonian ontology as a kind of model for what an ontology should involve. It should involve a location system, a basic class or classes of entities, and some kind of structuring relations that hold all these entities together in a single world. In setting out the ontology that is implicit in the discursive basis of the second cognitive revolution, we will need to find appropriate analogues to these parts of the Newtonian ontology for ours.

When something is said, does it matter very much where in physical space it is said? The commonsense answer is no, but it does matter a great deal who says it. What corresponds to Newtonian space in our scheme as a system of location for the basic entities of discursive psychology is an array of people. There is a people-space constituted by the individuals who can be speakers or counterspeakers or listeners. People are things specified something like spatial points, defined in terms of interpersonal, social, and political frameworks. The entities that occur at the people points, the "things" of the discursive world, are speech-acts. What corresponds to times in the scheme? It could be some sequence of utterances, actual speakings, that can serve as a basic rhythm on to which other speech-acts can be mapped. We can choose some sequence of speakings to define the flow of moments in discursive time. This time will prove to be largely independent of how the clock ticks.

Recent work on the problems faced by sufferers from Alzheimer's disease has shown that part of their difficulties with other people is simply a matter of the timing of speech. The results of this research are quite surprising. If you ask people, even the medical specialists who are dealing with the Alzheimer's patient, they will nearly always tell you that the sufferer has a mental defect, which is displayed in defective speech. Alzheimer's patients are then spoken to as if they are simpleminded or mere infants. With transcripts taken from a particular day-care center, Sabat (Sabat and Harré, 1992) showed that the utterances of the Alzheimer's sufferers can be put into a sequence, U1, U2, . . . U3, . . U4, and so on, in which certain time gaps, expressed by dots, appear. These gaps can be quite easily removed by editing with a tape recorder. If one now plays over this conversation without the gaps, it appears more or less normal. Conversations between the Alzheimer's patients and caretakers in places like day-care centers frequently fail because the interlocutor is irresistibly drawn to fill in the time gaps with what it seems the Alzheimer's patient should have then said next, not waiting for the sufferer to say it for themselves. The result is often unsatisfactory for both speakers. If one's speech is patterned by the conversation time of ordinary intercourse, which is usually fairly close to clock time, one cannot converse easily with an Alzheimer's patient. If one can manage to adopt their utterance time, one can converse more easily and normally. Of course, managing such a conversation is hard to start with, because the long pauses during which the Alzheimer's sufferer is finding the words are hard to bridge in silence.

The concept of *speech-act* also needs some spelling out. Austin introduced the term to emphasize the fact that when someone "issued an utterance" as he used to say, or performed a speech-action, the words were being used to perform three different acts. An utterance is certainly an action; that is, it is intentional, meant as something. It becomes a speech-act when it is taken up by the others to whom it has been addressed. Each speech-act has an illocutionary force, its social power as uttered in a certain context. Words can be meant as invitations, warnings, promises, threats, apologies, reprimands, congratulations, and so on. These are not descriptions of anything, but ways to do things. There is also the perlocutionary effect of the words to take into account, what is accomplished in their being taken up by others as a speech-act with a certain force. There are many acts that a particular form of words could accomplish. Depending on context and the nature and status of the people engaged in talk, a certain form of words, meant and taken up as a speech-act, might have the illocutionary force of an invitation and the perlocutionary effect of bringing about an engagement to marry. The very same form of words might on another occasion and in the mouths of other speakers be taken as occasion of offense as a sexual harassment. Perlocutionary effects only come about because an utterance has been taken to have a certain illocutionary force.

Analyzing discourse as sequences of acts is a very different matter than analyzing it in terms of the relations between true and false propositions. The work of the discursive psychologist is concerned predominantly with language in use as the accomplishment of acts or as attempts at their accomplishment.

What links speech-acts into psychologically relevant structures? According to the discursive view, there are a great variety of normative or regulating constraints on what can be meaningfully or properly said at any point in a conversation among persons of a certain type in contexts of specific character. The orderly structure of a conversation is maintained by norms of correctness and propriety. This is not a causal theory. In the physical world model, events and things are linked into structures and patterns by causal relations. But one speech-act does not cause another. Rather, one speech-act makes another appropriate or, as they say in this theory, normatively accountable. If someone says something with a certain illocutionary force, then the next thing is normatively accountable. For example, if somebody intends what they say as an invitation, and someone else takes it up as a question—that is, provides what could be taken as an answer—then the second speaker's utterance is incorrect, in accordance with the norms of usage of interrogative sentences in English. There are, however, occasions in which an account offered by the second speaker apropos of the seemingly nonstandard remark they made next can override the first speaker's intention and remake the whole conversation.

The crucial insight that enables us to explain psychological phenomena as patterns of discursive acts is that norms and rules emerging in historical and cultural circumstances operate to structure the things people do. If, for instance, we are building a psychology of emotions that can claim to be a part of a human science, or to understand, systematically, the significance of displays of personality or declarations of attitudes, we must come to see these as symbolic acts, and as normatively accountable. The explanatory task of psychology is to be defined by trying to answer the question: What it is that makes something right or wrong, the appropriate thing to feel, say, do, think, or experience?

The first theory of this sort, proposed for explaining social interactions, was the role-rule theory. It turned out to be only one of the many possible theories that we would need if we were to understand how conversations and other social interactions involving discursive practices are organized. The role-rule theory was far too rigid to serve as a general framework for social psychology. But it was clear that there were certain kinds of discursive events that were organized by something very like a role-rule system. In ceremonials and similar formal interactions, the roles of the people involved are relatively fixed, and the requirements for symbolic actions in that role are given, often in a formula. If the formulas are recited correctly, then the social act is accomplished. But as a general prescription for theories of social action, the role-rule schema was too static. In the late 1970s there was considerable criticism of the role-rule theory, on the grounds that real life is not so stereotyped as the use of ceremonials, as the source of models of social action would have required if it were to be viable as a general theory of social action.

A more recent development of the theory of normative accountability makes the dynamic transformations and multiple meanings of any sequence of actions central. Instead of roles and rules, which are rigid concepts, we substitute the notion of "position as a speaker" for "role." Instead of citing rules to account for the structure of a discursive interaction—say, a conversation—we use the idea of narrative conventions. This is a much more flexible idea. A narrative convention is simply an expression of the ways in which we tell stories in our culture. Narrative conventions, we should say, are like the "rules of grammar" of our native tongue, immanent in conversational practices. One does not learn the rules and then act in accordance with them. One learns the practice and then, for various purposes, one might extract some rules and use them to express the norms of that practice. Anthropologists have long been very familiar with this idea (Lévi-Strauss, 1972), the idea of the immanence of the norms of a culture in the storytelling practices of this or that tribe, including our own (Bruner, 1990), in which a culture is expressed.

The notion of position is a newcomer. It was first explicitly formulated as a psychological concept in certain radical feminist writings (Hollway, 1984). One important difference between the way different categories of people (for instance, men and women, adults and children, professors and students) enter into conversations can be expressed in terms of their rights and obligations to say certain kinds of things (that is, use certain categories of speech-acts). These rights and duties constitute "positions." For example, the concept of "position" has been used by feminist social psychologists to explain why it is that, in a mixed group, women say less than the men, whereas in groups of persons of the same sex, women say more to each other than men say to each other in their groups. The explanation offered is that women members of a mixed group are positioned as having lesser rights to criticize a male speaker than the men do. A position then is a set of rights, duties, and obligations as a speaker, particularly with respect to what we have called the illocutionary or social force of what one may say.

An important assumption in the general theory of discursive psychology is the principle that everything in the human world, both social/public and personal/private, is, in some measure, indeterminate. One can best see what this principle means by looking at some examples. The attitudes one expresses are usually quite vaguely specified: "I'm not very keen on Chinese food." But they can be made more or less determinate as the situation and the other people involved in an episode require: "I'll have Peking duck but not white mushrooms, thanks." The procedure for voting in an election is a practice by which those who take part are forced to display a determinate political attitude. Furthermore, as Averill (1982) and Pearce and Cronen (1981) have pointed out, it is always possible to renegotiate the perceived nature and type of almost any psychological phenomenon, including emotions, memories, opinions, decisions, intentions, motives, and so on, even what one has claimed to have seen. We make psychological phenomena, such as social acts, declarations of remembering, displays of attitudes, manifestations of emotions, and so on, determinate for certain purposes. These procedures of making determinate are invoked typically when what has happened has been challenged, particularly if something to do with personal honor or dignity hangs on it.

Positioning highlights the importance of "making something of a situation" as one participates in it and according to one's perceptions of it. This idea in turn underpins the concept of subjectivity, which expresses the way things appear to be or are signified by the speech and action of a person seen in relation to a discursive context. This is the closest our present approach comes to an account of the Cartesian "inner." That idea arises because even though

the meanings that inform our subjectivity arise in public discourse
they may or may not be expressed or even named by the subject.
If they are concealed or unexpressed then we can speak of the
privacy or internality of the mind. If they are not named, not made
explicit as meanings affecting one's behavior, then we can speak
of the unconscious. We shall pursue both topics in later chapters.

Conclusion

We have now laid out the main concepts of this approach to
psychology. We have explained the idea of an ontology in which
utterances, interpreted as speech-acts, become the primary entities
in which minds become personalized, as privatized discourses. In
this ontology, people are locations for discourses, both public and
private. Psychological time is related to utterances and other acts
of sign use, and not to clocks. The structure of the discourses in
which psychological phenomena, such as remembering, displays
of emotions, avowals of attitudes, attributions of causality and
responsibility, and so on, are created are under the control of
conventions of right and wrong performances. We have introduced
the idea of fluid positionings instead of fixed roles and noted the
importance of subjectivity as important contributions to understanding the diverse and changing rights and obligations that influence and explain our behavior as discursive agents.

❖ 3 ❖

Thoughts

Cognition and Thought

W hen we examine the ways in which psychology studies
thoughts and thinking, the essential functions of mind, we
find that we become enmeshed in experiments on what are called
cognitive processes. These have to do with the ways in which
patterns and complex stimuli are organized and recognized by a
person, the factors that affect recall of previously learned or encountered information, the understanding of language, and the
procedures that seem to be involved in human problem solving.
Before we start to explore some of this material, it would be as
well to try to say something about the relation between thought
and cognition. To do this we will need to focus on thoughts as we

normally understand them and then compare our findings with the available psychological approaches to cognition. This will lay a foundation for a discursive account of both thought and cognition.

Some Main Properties of Thoughts

It is often difficult to know where to begin discussing thought, in that what it is seems to be something mysterious and hidden from our common knowledge. Philosophers have said a number of things about thoughts that help us understand why thoughts are not quite the same thing as the commonly discussed "cognitive processes." If we start with a simple example, it is possible to identify some key features of thoughts. Consider the thought <that is a little newt>. It has at least five properties.

1. It shows *intentionality* in that it is *about* something (Brentano, 1973 [1924]). There are two aspects to this property. First, I think of the object of my thought according to a certain conception; thus, when I see the newt, I might not realize that I have seen an amphibian because I do not connect the two conceptions: <newt> and <amphibian>. Second, it is possible for an object of my thought, such as Pegasus, to be nonexistent as in <I wonder what Pegasus is doing>. These two features imply that saying what my thought is about involves more than just picking out some object in the world.

2. My thoughts figure in an *explanation of my behavior*. If I set out to catch a newt, then when I see the little brown thing beside the pool and think <that is a newt>, I will try to catch that thing. Thus my performance of the actions proper for catching newts is explained by my thought (Davidson, 1980).

3. For this link between thought and behavior to work, my thoughts ought to *"aim at"* the kind of appropriateness the situation calls for. If I am instructing someone in biology, I will aim (or ought to) aim at truth in my discursively presented "newt-thoughts." If I am warning someone about to step into the pool by

crying out, "Watch out for the newts!" I should aim at alerting them. If it is not true that the little brown thing is a newt, I will not succeed in the first task. (I might in the second.) Therefore, in thinking, I must try to master the criteria for what counts as a newt so that my thoughts about newts are, in general, appropriate. In that sense, there are rules and norms that "govern" thought (Gillett, 1992a).

4. When I express a thought, I do so by using some symbolic device, such as words, pictures, graphs, images, and so on. I can be said to understand a language or whatever symbolic system I am using when I am able to use its resources appropriately. Therefore there is an intimate link between *thought and the use of symbols and signs, including language.* In general, I can communicate my well-formed thoughts to others who understand my language (Davidson, 1984).

5. My thoughts are, if I choose, *private* to me. I need not let anybody else know the thoughts I entertain in the privacy of my own mind. For instance, if you were walking along the path with me and I did not want you to notice the newt, I might think to myself <that is a newt> but give no indication of doing so.

These features need to be related to our understanding of "cognition" and "discourse." We shall examine them in turn.

Intentionality

A thought is always about something. A convenient but ultimately dangerous way of discussing these matters is to introduce the word *concept* as a stand-in for the long-winded description of someone having command of a range of techniques for the use of a sign. Instead of saying, "NN has mastered the use of numerals," we can say "NN has acquired the 'concept of number.' " Though the terminology of concepts is useful, it is dangerous in this regard: It tends to suggest that there is some mysterious entity, "the concept of number," which NN now possesses. And of course the whole point of the discursive turn in cognitive psychology is to get away from mythical mental entities. The terminology of "concepts," however, does have one great virtue. It allows us to talk about the expression of thoughts without specifying which kind of device is being used at any moment. It could be a map, a word, a picture, a bodily feeling, and so on. It is in this generic sense that we shall be using the word *concept* in what follows.

Using this terminology, we can say that what a thought is about is given by the concepts that make up the thought, the words that make up the verbal expression of the thought, or the components of the picture, real or imagined, that one uses to think about newts. Thus the thought <that is a little brown newt> is made up in part by the concepts <little>, <brown>, and <newt> and is about something I have seen that is little, brown, and a newt. But concepts are not just "read off" the world; I have to understand and be able to use the words and other signs with which I express them. If, for instance, I do not understand the concept <newt>—that is, have no mastery of the word *newt* or grasp of the use of a suitable picture or the like—then I cannot think of the little brown thing as being a newt. Because I can only think of the object in ways that depend on my grasp of signs, both verbal and iconic or pictorial, it is not sufficient to say, as some might do, that thoughts arise solely from the impingement of objects on the senses of thinkers. To mark this fact, we contrast *intentional* aspects of thoughts with the *extensional* specifications of the objects and features of the environment that they concern. A thought is considered under its extensional aspect when the class of things that it is about is specified simply by listing the objects and features comprehended by the term. Extensional specifications are in fact problematic in a way that is often overlooked by psychologists.

It is difficult to pick out an object to enter into the list of objects that belong to some kind of thing without drawing on some meaningful discourse in which the typical properties of such a thing are laid out or assumed. To pick something out as a newt, one must look for something that is an amphibian, an animal, a moving thing, and so on. Every thought picks out the object in some specific way that determines what I can go on to think about it and do with it (Fodor, 1968). For instance, if my aim is to catch a newt but I do not realize that the little brown thing in the pond is a newt, then I will not go on to try to catch *it*. We sometimes refer to this as "referential opacity." A thought may be opaque in that I may not be able to see beyond the way the thing is specified in that thought and realize that I am thinking of the same object, which, in another thought, is presented in another guise. So I may not realize that when someone is talking about Trinity Pudding they are talking about the same dish I would be talking about if I used the expression *crème brûlée*. For this reason, an account of thoughts that focuses just on objects or physical stimulus conditions and does not pay attention to the various ways that we might think about them—that is, the various signs or words we might use in that thinking, and how we might use them—will not suffice to explain behavior. Thus the intentionality of thought will be a central part of any adequate account of cognitive processes.

Thoughts in the Explanation of Behavior

The way a person thinks about objects informs and guides his or her behavior in a way that the concept <ticket> makes even more vivid than the <newt> example. Imagine that a person is given a small piece of paper with some printing on it. In the absence of any experience with tickets, or instruction in the way the word *ticket* is used, the meaning of the concept <ticket> will be beyond the grasp of that person, who will be unable to use the piece of paper in the way it is meant to be used. Any account of thought ought to make it clear how this physical object can figure in explanations of the complex behavior that follows from its being regarded as a ticket. This example makes it clear how applying a concept to something enables me to act in ways that otherwise I could not. Even if you knew that I was attending to the ticket and that my visual apparatus was intact, you would not necessarily understand my actions until you were told, "He realizes [or perhaps thinks] that it is a ticket." Therefore it is my conception of an object and the concepts I apply to it that, by and large, explain my behavior toward it (not just specifying which object it is). This conceptualizing of the thing involves far more than detecting a pattern in the light or doing a series of computations based on those patterns of "information" (a concept of notable slipperiness, to which we shall return). Our view will be that we cannot understand the conceptualization of the ticket without locating what someone does with it or says about it in the relevant discourses where tickets occupy a meaningful place.

Truth and Appropriateness

"The world is independent of my will," said Wittgenstein (1961 [1922]). He was wrong, of course, because what I do can change the world in a number of ways, sometimes just as I intended. But he was pointing to the fact that what I think about the world ought to be guided by what is true of the world and not just by what I wish it were like. Thus I try, in thought, to *fit* my thoughts to the world (of this, more later) and, on that basis, to formulate ways to act that will achieve my goals (indeed, for human beings, knowing more about the world is often a goal in itself). Of course I must also try to fit my thoughts to the cultural conventions of the place and the time I live, so that my actions and sayings will be appropriate. Not least I must cast them in the local language. (Knowing more about local conventions can also be a goal for human beings.) The problem for traditional theories is to get over the barrier that seems to separate the thinker's mind from the world.

In the view of thought and knowledge prevalent in much of philosophy and psychology, thinkers are presented as trapped behind a *veil of perception* that consists of "what their senses tell them" (Hacker, 1991, p. 145). In this view of the mind as an inner realm of images and calculations, I can never get past this veil to check and see whether my thoughts really do match what is "out there." What is more, as Wittgenstein realized, such private experiences could not be the roots of a language because, if they were, I would never know what you meant or were referring to when you said anything and you would never be able to know what I was referring to. Obviously the things that fix the meanings of words cannot be hidden inside the respective heads of different people or else we would each be uncertain all the time what anybody else was talking about. Thus it is hard to say what I could mean by claiming that my thoughts are true, and my utterances meaningful, if I am trapped within them and at their mercy (and they are hidden inside me). The problem runs very deep because others cannot get outside their veils of perception either. This entails that none of us knows what the world is really like, nor what others think, nor whether anything we think is actually true, nor what anyone else means by the words they use, nor indeed what I mean by the words I use. Clearly, we have to find some way to make sense of the fact that we *can* aim to think true thoughts and express them in a common system of signs. This is an even more pressing need when we consider the fact that thoughts are communicable.

Thought and Symbolic Systems, Including Language

Thinking is, by and large, communicable. In fact, one of the most impressive things about human beings is the way they can "pool" their thoughts to achieve things that would be impossible for them to do as individuals. If we accept that a very basic part of our thinking is to do with using words in a way that makes for the possibility of a common language, there must be a way for us to compare the basis on which I think something with the basis on which you think it or there could be no way for us to agree that what was by the pool was, say, a newt, or for me to teach you that the concept <newt> applied to things like that. The fact of communicability implies that there are systematic and essential links between my use of any concept (like <newt>) and your use of it. They must be systematic, so that we can use the links between our thoughts at different times and places to build up a knowledge of the world, integrate our experience into a coherent whole, and develop successful strategies for coping with the situations we meet. And the links must be essential, or fundamental to the nature of thinking, because they have to do with the basic building blocks of thought—shared concepts and their use in developing cognitive skills through language teaching and learning.

The communicability of thoughts is secured by the mutual intelligibility of a shared symbolic system, such as a common language. Notice that even in the traditional view there is an intimate "link" between language and thought, that the former is the medium for the expression of the latter and secures the relationship between thinking and the appropriateness of my actions expressing or realizing those thoughts. If I know when something would be called a "ticket," then I know what tickets are and can use that knowledge in a consistent and fruitful way in my theatergoing and train-traveling activities. Although this (traditional) "link" does not entail that every thought must be articulated in terms of understanding a language, it does imply that there is a close relationship between the use of language and the grasp of the concepts in which thoughts are articulated. In particular, it implies that a thinker learns the rules as to what counts as an item of a given type by mastering the use of the linguistic terms that express the concept referring to that type (e.g., <newt> or <ticket>).

This line of thought is highly congenial to psychologists who follow Vygotsky (1962). He argued that the cognition of a child took shape in the context of language use in conversational interactions with adults and thus that thought and language were inextricably linked. Vygotsky claimed that "the system of signs restructures the whole psychological process" (1962, p. 35). He highlights the role of the skilful use of *publicly* meaningful signs at the very center of everything we would include under the category of human thought.

Private Thoughts

When I saw the newt, I might have decided to "keep my thoughts to myself." To do this I must keep a straight face and "hold my tongue." It is characteristic of thoughts that I can do this. In fact, one's "innermost thoughts" may never be explained or expressed to anybody else. But, if this is so, how can we claim that there is an essential link between language and thought? Thoughts must, in some sense, and for those who mastered the art of concealment, be private. But if this is so, how can we claim that there is an essential link between language and thought? Surely, I can think what I want to without saying anything about it.

We cannot resolve this impasse unless we abandon the idea that the distinctive properties of any psychological phenomenon are (necessary and sufficient) conditions that must attend every instance of that phenomenon. The easiest way to understand this relationship is by considering the related connection between meaning and truth. In learning a language, I must initially try to obey the rules quite carefully. Thus, in relation to factual or descriptive statements, I must correctly signify objects and their properties and give expression to those significations or, in other words, speak what I take to be true about them. My understanding of the meanings of terms and expressions can be built on this grasp of truth or validated signification and how to express it in a given discourse. As the others participating in a discourse correct my usage and I come to an understanding of the meanings available in that discourse, I become able to deceive them by using terms in ways that depend upon correct usage but do not express my thoughts. In a similar way, my ability to pick out, say, frogs as frogs may be built upon my public use of the relevant term *frog,* but I can grow out of the need to be so open in my thoughts about the world. Having once mastered the basic tools of thought, I can construct thoughts for my own private use and outstrip any need to make manifest what I am thinking.

Thus the trick of hiding what I think does not undermine the suggested link, because what I am hiding is an activity that has grown out of and reflects my interactions with other thinker/speakers and the world we share, in particular that repertoire of discursive practices that, as Vygotsky pointed out, serves to give form to the otherwise inchoate content of the individual mind (activity of the individual person).

The Contents of Thoughts

Some writers use the terms *content of thought* or *mental content* in such a way as to suggest that there are pictures or bits of language in the mind, and that thought is a kind of operation on those inner things (Sajama and Kamppinen, 1987). This is obviously faulty because it would be absurd to say that someone was not thinking when they were cogitating about something unpicturable, such as the famous chiliagon (a regular geometrical figure with a thousand angles) or nonlinguistic (such as the aroma of coffee)! Another, more conceptualist approach starts with the idea that a thought like <that frog is green> seems to "contain" its component concepts, say, <that frog> and <green>, as its constituent parts. In forming the thought a person is mentally capturing *that frog* and linking it to a color concept <green>. This is why some writers have said that forming thoughts involves subsuming objects under concepts. The structure of a thought in this view bears a suggestive relationship to the structure of declarative sentences that have a subject and a predicate (either of which can be indicated by more than one word).

Other writers talk as if all thoughts were little word-pictures of states of affairs in the world and could be described in this kind of way. But this will not account for the difference between the thought of wanting a certain state of affairs to obtain in the future and the thought of regretting that such a state of affairs obtained in the past! And, of course, there are many thoughts such as <I wonder what *that* is?>; <Shall I compare thee to a summer's day?>; <5 + 7 = 12>, and so on that are not of this descriptive, object-concept form. What is more, even if thoughts were sentences or pictures in my head (so that there was a Language of Thought other than one's native tongue), we would still have to say how subjects could imbue those sentences, word-pictures, or images with meanings or contents. This is a profound problem that Wittgenstein clearly identified (Kenny, 1991).

If I am trying to explain the use of signs or symbols in the public realm, it is no advance if I merely shift to signs or symbols in the private ("internal") realm. It remains to be explained what it is to understand the "internal" signs or symbols. This, we have suggested, is a matter of studying the techniques and skills of thinkers involved in various kinds of discourse. But if these skills are what is essential, then what function is performed by the inner "pictures"?

However we come to understand them, one influential metaphor for thought contents is to imagine them as composite somethings made up by combining conceptions of objects and general concepts in such a way as to build up what we might call a cognitive map of the world around us—as containing a round pond over there, a clump of yellow flowers next to it, a dog that is spotted, and so on. Furthermore, the metaphor can be extended to include the idea that conceptions of objects are themselves, by and large, made up of yet more fundamental concepts. Thus <that spotted dog> is made up of <spotted> and <dog>; <the rotten oak>, of <rotten> and <oak>; and so on. Whatever way we choose to understand thoughts, concepts are important and we have already noted that concepts and their meanings are discerned as we locate them in the discourses where they are used.

Even as we think in this way, however, we should realize that concepts are a way of describing the stabilized uses of signs and symbols. Once again, we should note the convenience of the terminology, and at the same time we should guard against slipping into thinking that as well as signs in use there are also concepts in the head.

At this point we can understand another fact about concepts that is directly relevant to psychological theories of cognition. Concepts confer an inference-making ability on those who grasp them. As soon as you become aware that what is before you is a handle then you are set to make certain other moves in thought such as <where there is a handle there might be a door>, <a door might lead out of this room>, <turning that handle may be the way to escape>. It is this property of concepts that allows us to construct not only simple trains of reasoning but complex theories about the world built up in terms of conceptual links between the things we observe and do. These complex constructions in thought allow bridge building between different sets of discursive skills. Thus, for instance, thinking of a frog as an animal allows us to react to it in ways reserved for biological rather than mechanically driven objects. At a more complex level, thinking of personality as being made up of dimensions allows us to calculate such things as the weightings of different factors in trying to understand a person.

At the heart of this activity are the thinkers themselves as they are located in certain discourses (Gillett, 1992b). It should be evident from what we have said that thinkers as concept users (competent managers of systems of signs) are active participants in experience. They select what aspects of a situation to attend to and these become a basis for the use of certain (words) [concepts]; they apply these (words) [concepts] and then can reason about the experience and link it to other experiences and more abstract thoughts. Thus the grasp of (the use of a word) [a concept] is an active discursive skill. It is selective in the face of a rich set of experiential possibilities. It is built on participation in discourse, and it is governed by rules or prescriptive norms that tell the thinker what counts as an item of this or that type (e.g., what counts as a *dog* in the fireplace or in the kennel, a *frog* in the pond or in the throat, or a *heavy metal band* in the dance hall or around the ankle).

Thinkers' awareness of these rules shows in their recognition that there is a right and a wrong way to capture in thought the object or property that is thought about. Of course, when we read the terms *right* and *wrong,* we are immediately alerted to the idea of discourse as a locus of norms and proper and improper relationships that shape the subjectivities and activities of individuals.

Conclusion

This analysis of thoughts has told us a number of things about their basic features. Thoughts are *intentional,* in the sense that they are about things or are directed to ends that arise in human activity. They are, at heart, communicable; other signs (concepts) are learned as we deal with things around us in the presence and with the help of others. As we do this, we latch on to the skills of referring to them and isolating their common features that are made available by the other people who train us to use them. Thoughts play a part in the *explanation of behavior* because they account for the links anyone makes between their present and past experiences, and these links (or the words and signs [concepts] that capture them) shape their activity in present experiences. Thoughts have a *link to truth* because to be successful one must master the trick of thinking of the world as it really is (using terms and expressions in their validated ways), not just as one might wish it to be. *Language* and thought are tied to one another because talk about thought is a way of talking about discursive activity. Thought has rule-governed or normative features because the rules governing the proper ways to group things and to identify their interesting features actually exist within the use of the terms of a language.

Thus the elements of thought arise between different thinkers and can be communicated about (which is why a reader of this text has a chance to understand the thoughts that are expressed in it). But thought is not an overt operation on the world and therefore, once the terms and elements have been mastered, the contents of one's thoughts can be hidden from other people. In this sense, thoughts are potentially *private*, constructed apart from the dealings we have with the things they are about although dependent on our past dealings with those things. Thoughts, then, are not objects in the mind but the activity and essence of mind. They reside in the uses we are making of public and private systems of signs. To be able to think is to be a skilled user of these sign systems, that is, to be capable of managing them correctly.

❖ 4 ❖

Cognitive Psychology of the First Kind

*It is misleading then to talk of thinking as a mental
activity. We may say that thinking is essentially the
activity of operating with signs.*

Wittgenstein

Cognition

When psychologists realized that the study of behavior and
its relation to physical specified conditions would not suffice for an understanding of what human beings do, they began
to try to look at the processes in the mental "black box" that
were supposed to intervene between stimulus-input and behav-
ioral-output. The study of these processes was to be the focus of
cognitive psychology, the program that we have called the First
Cognitive Revolution. Neisser outlines the topic of this kind of
cognitive psychology as follows:

"Cognition" refers to all the processes by which the sensory input is transformed, reduced, elaborated, stored, recovered, and used. It is concerned with these processes even when they operate in the absence of relevant stimulations, as in images and hallucinations. Such terms as sensation, perception, imagery, retention, recall, problem-solving, and thinking, among many others, refer to hypothetical stages or aspects of cognition. (Neisser, 1967, p. 4)

Two things are immediately clear from this outline. It is assumed without any argument that the "stages or aspects of cognition" are *mental* entities. It is also clear that thoughts or thinking and cognitive processes, as defined here, are not quite the same thing. Thoughts have objects of which a person can give an account; they encompass our reasons for behaving thus and so; they aim at truth and propriety; and whereas they can be expressed linguistically, they may be intentionally hidden from others. These properties locate people's thoughts in the discourses that affect them and inform their understanding of self and others.

But many processes that are involved in the transformation of sensory input will not be of this kind. For instance, the targeting functions that compare the trajectory of a limb with that of its moving target so as to allow a smooth interception are, in Neisser's definition, part of cognition although they are performed by the cerebellum and might, in other definitions, be regarded as part of the motor fine-tuning mechanism of the brain. It is just this ambiguity that leads one to interpret the findings of cognitive science more carefully than is usually done. The final clarification of this issue will emerge only when we have shown how models are used in the development of cognitive theories as well as the inevitable, but fruitful, ambiguities in their interpretations.

Consider, for instance, the way in which a rapidly directed set of eye movements is used to scan presented stimuli so as to enable them to be perceptually categorized. Although the pattern of eye movements is part of the skilled performance involved in determining categorizations and therefore serves purposes shaped in discourse, it is not comfortably assimilated to thought. Thinking

about how one might categorize something is a process of a quite
different kind, not least because it is accomplished discursively.

Finally, consider the ability to kick a football with the velocity
and direction needed to go over the goalkeeper's defending hands
but under the crossbar and into the goal. This performance is
clearly "cognitive" within the definition given above but is not
accomplished by means that can be evaluated for truth or propriety. Like any skilled action, it is evaluated by the degree to which
it serves to accomplish the striker's project. In fact, the more one
thinks about what is involved in doing such a thing and the calculations that would be required to accomplish it discursively, the
more impossible it seems for anyone to get it right in the brief
moment one has to size up the shot and strike the ball.

We must therefore conclude that not everything that intervenes
between input to the brain and output from musculature is part of
thinking. Making models of possible mechanisms by which information is processed will tell us about the component microskills
that go into our being the kind of creatures who can think thoughts
and use discourse-based rules to adapt to our world. The most we
can really hope for from a cognitive psychology, as Neisser (1967)
defines it, is that it will reveal the complex functions that underpin
activities such as attending to, thinking about, believing, recognizing, desiring, intending, and so on. The essential ambiguity of
models of cognition leaves open the question of whether these
models are abstract representations of structures and processes in
the brain and nervous system or whether they are metaphorical
presentations of the "grammatical" (that is, discursively grounded) structure and relationships of intended, goal-directed, and
norm-constrained human action. Sometimes a model may allow
both interpretations. The distinction should be made case by case
and cannot, in the nature of the matter, be solved in general, nor
can any one mode of interpretation be prescribed universally for
all cases.

We should also note that many of our psychological terms are
locked into this intentional discourse (concerning beliefs, intentions, and so on). These terms express concepts like evidence,

inference, conclusion, decision, and even information. But in order to discuss these we will need to look at rule-governed discursive activity and not at physical systems in which things such as excitations, triggering, differential stimulation, inhibition, and so on occur. If we want to discuss mechanisms that use processes of this kind, we will have to be scientifically honest. We may derive good specifications of such processes from intense study of simple transitions and relationships between physical types and behavioral types but we should be sensitive to the points at which we import assumptions based on the familiarity of the interpersonal skills evident in language games and discourses to do the real work of cognitive explanation (Kenny, 1991). For instance, if we claim that a sharp spatial change in retinal illumination provides evidence for an edge, we usually mean that it excites a cluster of brain cells that fire when a person sees an edge, and we have not yet solved the problem of what it is for a person to see an edge. If we keep these distinctions clearly in mind then we might well find some interesting resonances between cognitive and thought-based explanations. But it remains to be seen whether an adequate psychology should abandon the latter for the former (Stich, 1983).

Therefore, as we turn our attention to the kinds of things that we are told by cognitive science, we will try to detect those things properly explained by adverting to the discursive contexts within which behavior has been shaped, and distinguish these from functions that take place at what we might call a "subdiscursive" level and that, though not discursive per se, might be thought of as contributing to those broader adaptive strategies that discursively structure human behavior because they involve thoughts, intentions, and so on. In fact, just such a distinction seems implicit in certain cautions offered by Allport in his discussion of neuropsychological evidence concerning the relation between language and cognition.

> There is not some subprocess, nor any collection of subprocesses, called "perception" (for example) that we could separate off from other subprocesses called "memory," "attention," "reasoning," still less

from "intelligence": nor vice versa. In other words, these descriptive
faculties are not parts of the mind. They do not partition its structure. . . . many different constituent processes interact, in overlapping
combinations, to make them. (Allport, 1983, p. 72)

Modestly interpreted, Allport is arguing that the competencies
we find evident in discourse, which engage with terms like *knowledge, belief, responsibility, decision, intention, action,* and so on,
are not to be equated with the kinds of function that characterize
traditional models of cognitive processes. This having been said,
it remains open to those who are interested in discourse to prefer
the terms *mind* and *thought* and to leave terms like *information
processing system* and *cognition* to cognitive psychologists interested in functions with different (nonepistemic or nonnormative)
properties. The latter could only be functions of the brain and
nervous system. Once again it is the inherent dualism of interpretations of the models of cognition that leaves open the slide from
the usual meaning of *cognitive,* that is, "pertaining to thought," to
a new meaning: namely, "pertaining to brain processes," that is,
"not pertaining to thought." These slips and slides occur in the
sciences from time to time and must be carefully recorded to avoid
transferring aspects of the old uses to the new. Yet the danger of
misinterpretation must be run, because it is just those ambiguities
that make cognitive models fruitful.

Having made these points, we can look at current work in cognitive psychology to try to discern how discursive psychology might
or might not be able to reformulate the implicit questions.

Some Fragments of Empirical Cognitive Psychology

Discursive psychology would be particularly interested in those
areas where discursive skills and competencies inform the way in
which human beings use *information,* in the nontechnical sense of
that multivocal term. Allport (1983) reports on the way in which
people recall the content of speech-acts. This recall involves "a

representation that is wholly independent of the original linguistic construction and wording, and in which inferences made by the subject are not subsequently distinguished from propositions contained in the original text" (Allport, 1983, p. 70). This is a familiar phenomenon for those of us who use more than one language. One may not know which language a certain piece of information was presented in. Allport concludes that it is the significance or meaningfulness of what is recalled that determines the way a person retains and uses the content of an essentially language-based experience. But he is at pains to prove that this meaning is not some formal reflection of the language actually used and that its understanding is based in broader real-life competencies.

> There can be no language understanding without the appropriate . . . framework of prior knowledge about the subject of discourse, into which the new information can be integrated and from which missing information can be inferred. (Allport, 1983, p. 71)

We would interpret this as reflecting the fact that meaning and understanding reflect discursive contexts and forms of life and not just propositional structures with meanings that exist in relation to language alone. In fact, Allport also reports an experiment explicitly and successfully designed to show that

> the cognitive codes representing word-meanings are not, in any way, language- or word-specific. In particular there is no one-to-one correspondence between cognitive codes and individual lexemes, or words in the language. (Allport, 1983, p. 87)

The experiment involved several phases in which the competence of a brain-damaged subject in relation to written or spoken words and word meanings was examined. It emerged that the patient could not make selective spoken-to-written transitions for words with closely similar functional meanings (such as *dress* versus *frock*), nor could he make such transitions using nonsense words, nor could he make them with words having primarily intralinguistic or nonreferential uses (such as *some, all, she, under*) but he could make selective transitions accurately when words that differed significantly in meaning were used (e.g., *dress* and *sock*). We could therefore describe a pattern of losses in which words could not be distinguished on the basis of their linguistic or lexical form alone but required there to be a difference in their contextual meanings or references to a type or category of thing. One would expect, if words are given meaning by their use in real contexts where they signify things of interest to human subjects, that the cognitive system would not necessarily involve any quasi-linguistic central processing structure (we shall return to this in discussing formal and informal models of cognition). In fact, one could hardly have hoped for a more striking empirical demonstration of the correctness of Wittgenstein's account of meaning in the *Philosophical Investigations* (1953). At the same time, one trembles at the possibilities of imagining all sorts of bogus entities that are immanent in such daring metaphors as "cognitive codes representing word-meanings"!

Another interesting piece of data comes from the debate between advocates of analogical and propositional representation. Paivio (1971) found that subjects given sets of pictures or lists of words to memorize tended more readily to recall the pictures than the words. He explained this by using a dual-code theory wherein the pictures could be represented either in terms of their pictorial (nonverbal) or descriptive (verbal) content (or both) and so accessed by two distinct cognitive systems. Discourse analysis would look at this phenomenon slightly differently. We would take the view that the links to discursive situations are more open ended and, to some extent, more natural for pictures than for words, which have only their verbal form to locate them in the mind. Now, even if discourse, involving language and other arbitrary sign systems, is basic in the organization of much of our meaningful activity, we might suspect that more cues for recall would arise from a picture that immediately evokes a rich discursive situation than from a word that has an entirely conventional connection to what it signifies. We should also recall that not all meanings can be pictured in a simple way and so there might be differences if we attempted to look at "difficult" images such as those connected with words like *myth, beauty, relationship*, and so on. Therefore the reported effect may be specific to words and pictures of relatively easily recognized concrete objects. Of course the experiment only makes sense if we presume, as Wittgenstein reminds us on many occasions, that the subjects know how to take the pictures, that is, how to use a picture discursively.

A particularly telling fact in this regard is the observation by Pylyshyn (1979) that partial forgetting of "images" involves meaningful aspects or parts of those images. This suggests that an image is held together by its meaning-structure rather than by a pictorial similarity to states of affairs in the world. This is exactly what one would expect if discourse and signification were pervasive in representation (even if those representations and cognitive competencies are potentially separable from their explicitly linguistic signs once established, as Allport, 1983, suggests).

Pylyshyn (1984) has a further set of arguments to do with what he calls "cognitive penetrability." He notes that beliefs, desires, and other intentional aspects of human activity can structure or restructure our apparently imagistic recollections. This is yet more grist to the discursive mill. And here we are not saying that words, per se, structure cognition but merely that discourse, a significant part in which is played by the communicative use of signs and symbols, pictures, and words in use, is the medium in which cognitive activity takes shape.

Memory

Consider next the various distinctions, none of which is simply intertranslatable, made in research on long-term memory. These concern the differences between semantic and episodic memory, procedural and declarative memory, and explicit and implicit memory. Each distinction tends to be defined in relation to a specific set of tasks and instructions that, for discursive theory, would all be significant. We can make one fairly general observation and suggestion, however. It is widely recognized that episodic memory is more vulnerable than semantic memory to factors disrupting psychological competence (such as brain damage). The difference can be defined as follows:

> Semantic memory refers [to] our de-contextualised memory for facts about the entities and relations between entities in the world; for instance, that birds have wings and that a canary is a bird. In contrast episodic memory refers to knowledge about episodes and events, to entities that are marked as happening at a particular time. (Eysenck and Keane, 1990, p. 250)

These two aspects of memory are no longer considered to be completely separable. However, their differential vulnerability would indicate that one involves a more elaborate set of cognitive operations than the other. In fact, it is evident that this must be so. If, through participation in discourse, we develop skills of signifying types of things, individual things, and the relations between things, it would be a further achievement to locate a particular signified state of affairs in some overarching organization of one's place in the world so as to be able to remember an episode.

Whereas in a discursive analysis of mind this memorial phenomenon is understandable, we need to deepen the inquiry in two directions, one discursive and the other based in "information" processing theory, that is, in a theory of brain function. On the one hand, it would be interesting to map intentionally explicable points of readiness or resistance to so locate an experience—this would be a discursive inquiry. On the other hand, one would also like to be able to understand how the cognitive system takes information, structured according to its fit with different types of discursive events, and packages it according to a locatable individual instance of presentation rather than according to its conformity to general discursive categories. Both abilities (semantic and episodic) must contribute to a cognitive map (as we have already noted), but how our "information" processing system does the latter trick is and ought to be of distinct interest to cognitive scientists. Notice that the neuropsychological question is clarified and sharpened by a discursive analysis.

The general topic of problem solving is the last on which we shall touch in this sample of some areas of cognitive psychology.

Gestalt Expert Knowledge, Analogical Reasoning, Representational Redescription

In her model of cognitive development and problem solving, Karmiloff-Smith (1986, p. 110) describes several phases of problem-solving competence. She calls the first phase "procedural success," and that is all it involves, for instance, learning to pick hexagons from an array of geometric figures. The second phase is consolidation and stabilizing of the connections and links between elements of the task that led to success. This gives the subject control over the performance as a structured system of organized representations, but it also means, for instance, that the child introduces bits of speech into utterances where they are not needed or would treat each block in a construction task as a separate gravitational unit. The third phase is a comparative phase in which the connected structure of skills and representations of the task is linked into an adequate and explicit systematic representation of the wider discursive domain relevant to task mastery. Thus, in relation to our two examples, parts of speech would be used properly according to grammatical context, and block constructions respect holistic gravitational relations (for instance, in building a tower). Her conclusion is deeply congenial to a discursive analysis of cognition:

> Consciousness is an emergent property of the overall cognitive system and of its processes of gradual representational explication. (Karmiloff-Smith, 1986, p. 140)

Her view is that, by making explicit the skills involved in problem solving or mastery of a domain of cognitive techniques, a child renders those cognitive elements conscious. The point has been made the basis of an empirical technique by von Cranach (von Cranach and Harré, 1981). He showed how the disruption of a smoothly articulated set of actions necessary to accomplish a task led the participants in his experiments to formulate the rules of procedure explicitly. This implies that locating the elements and operations of a task in a discursive structure is the level toward which cognitive development moves. If we recall the norms and judgments that form part of a discourse, it becomes clear that the posited highest level of cognitive skill is one that merges signification, involving the appreciation and use of (interpersonal) evaluative judgments, with the skills in play in achieving procedural success and initial representation.

Conclusion

The problem with cognitive psychology as so conceived is the assumption of the existence of mental states and processes, "behind" the mental states and processes of our discursive activities. These mystery processes are invoked as explanations of discursive and practical activities in much the same way as "the dance of the molecules" is invoked as an explanation of the behavior of gases. Whereas molecules are real entities, constitutive of gases, these alleged unconscious mental states and processes are redundant. We have no reason to believe in their existence. How do they come to seem to be needed? The answer lies in the dual interpretations that can be made of cognitive models of mental activity. They can either be taken as formal representations of the "grammars" of the discursive activities we can record and study, or they can be taken as schematic representations of the brain and neural processes necessary to the implementation of our intentions and rules of procedure. In the next chapter we shall explain the nature and uses of models in the sciences and show how this dual interpretation, which is the essence of fruitful model construction, must be firmly adhered to. The holding operation allows us to resist the temptation to suppose that cognitive psychology is based on picturing the (mythical) "inner mechanism of the mind."

❖ 5 ❖

Cognitive Modeling

Models in Natural Science and in Psychology

In the last chapter we found ourselves making use of the notion of a "model," either in quotations from others or in explaining some finding from cognitive science. The essential ambiguity of models (in that they are capable of interpretation, either as ways of understanding or as pictures of things we cannot observe) is a matter of considerable importance. To understand the role of models, one must examine them on home territory, so to speak, in the physical sciences. It is now generally agreed that the heart of any scientific treatment of a field of phenomena is a central model. Model-making is one of those activities to which natural scientists are so accustomed that they rarely pause to ask themselves just

how they create models and assess models and how their models
are related to the realities they represent. Models, as they are used
in the natural sciences, are virtual or imagined systems, bearing
varying degrees of relevant similarity to aspects of the real world
they represent. Perhaps the best way to make clear the rather complex relations that models bear to reality on the one hand and to
the basic theories of a discipline on the other is to describe two
simple cases: one of a model in use in the physical sciences and the
other in psychology.

The kinetic theory of gases is based on a central model of the
unobservable constitution of gases. According to the *molecular
model* of gases, gases are imagined to consist of swarms of minute
material bodies, "molecules." The terms with which physicists describe this model, such as "p" and "mc^2," have dual semantics. On
the one hand, the model is used to represent the unobserved behavior of the unobservable minute constituents of gases, and in
that role "p" is read as "rate of change of momentum at a phase
boundary" and "nmc^2" as the kinetic energy of the moving molecules. On the other hand, the model is used to abstract salient
observable properties of gases. Considered in that role, "p" is read
as "pressure," and "nmc^2" as temperature. In this way the general
gas law, derived by Boyle and Gay-Lussac from their experiments
on the relations between pressure, volume, and temperature of
gases ($PV = RT$), is interpreted in the model. On the other hand,
the molecular model ties together the observed behavior of gases
and the theoretical picture of what a gas might really consist of.

How did Clausius, Maxwell, and Boltzmann, the architects of
the kinetic theory, know how to construct their molecular model?
It certainly was not by observing molecules! There are various
ways of expressing the basic cognitive operations required but the
simplest and most illuminating is to express the relation between
a model and the various realities that it models by means of a
type-hierarchy. In this case the supertype is "Newtonian material
objects and their modes of interaction," the science of which is
well established in mechanics. By imagining their molecules as tiny
Newtonian particles (that is, a subtype of the Newtonian super-

type), the three great physicists helped themselves to the laws of Newtonian mechanics as at least part of the cluster of laws that could be used to describe their imagined world of molecules. Then Boltzmann made the final step by arguing that the real constituents of gases were also subtypes of the Newtonian supertype and therefore analogous to the molecules he and the others had imagined in their model, so that the model was seen both as a theory and as a picture (Way, 1992).

The drive theory of motivation will serve us for a simple psychological model to illustrate the use of models in the human sciences. If we imagine that behavior is controlled by "drives," which are like reservoirs of water building up until they find release, we can again achieve two purposes. On the one hand, we can picture a frenzy of internal electricitylike energy waiting to be discharged through circuits in the nervous system. On the other hand, we can do mathematical calculations on tendencies to behave in certain ways when one or other factor in the environment (like the availability of food) is changed for certain periods of time.

In its analytical employment a model serves to control the abstraction of features from the complex phenomena that are observed to occur in some field of interest. In its explanatory employment a model serves to represent the unobservable processes that are responsible for bringing those phenomena about. It is vital to understand that the terms of the model are subject to *dual interpretation*, once as observable properties of phenomena and once as unobservable properties of the processes responsible for those phenomena: "p" is at once "observed pressure" of a confined gas and "rate of change of momentum" of molecular particles as they strike the walls of the container. The model allows us to infer that observed pressure is caused by the impact of the moving molecules, without our needing to observe them!

A theory is just a description of the nature and workings of a model. There are all kinds of subtle points about model use that need not detain us here. The main thing is that we should be aware of the role of the model in linking a field of observed phenomena with the unobserved processes that produce those phenomena. It is vital to the reading of a model to identify the type-hierarchy in which it is embedded as a subtype. Only then can we properly interpret its double semantics. In general philosophy we would call the supertype of a relevant type-hierarchy an expression of the ontology of the science, that is, of the kinds of beings that the scientific community believes their world consists of.

We can now see how a model in cognitive science has an essential ambiguity. Is it a representation of the abstract forms of the phenomena under study, that is, a metaphorical representation of the grammar of the discursive procedures through which a cognitive task is routinely performed, or is it a model of the brain processes through which that performance is materially implemented, or is it, on occasion, both?

Theories of Cognitive Processes

The most influential theories of cognitive function have been formal theories based on the computer modeling of information use. To assess their value and to interpret their place in psychology, we need to deploy the insights into the use of models that we have gained by looking at the way models are constructed and employed in the physical sciences. These theories concentrate on specifiable states whose parameters are denumerable and codifiable in advance.

Suppose we have a problem in which there is a describable starting state comprising a set of elements each of which can be determined as being present or absent. For instance, relays a, b, and c may be ON, and d and e, OFF, in an information circuit. On the basis of this configuration of data points, the system can then make certain transitions to other states that have characteristics in common with a goal state (usually specified in advance). Thus, given the coded instruction "SWITCH OFF," the system goes to the state [a, b, ON; c, d, e, OFF]. The nature of the process is often described in terms of *states* and *rules* but the meanings of these terms are not quite as we have outlined in discussing thought and discourse. The states are structured sets of data able to be described in a way that fully captures their properties in relation to some system, but which system? States as described here are different than states that occupy locations in discourse (such as <believing in the integrity of the court system> or <having a tendency to defer to authority>). And the rules connecting the states are not like those we find in discursive contexts. Indeed, they are not rules at all; rather, they are procedures defined over a specifiable set of data points (such as SWITCH c OFF!). For such procedures we may, though at our peril, use the term *rule* as a metaphor. The procedure specifies just which transformations of the data will occur at each point and, by some means, makes the system change into the goal state. This has serious implications for the ability of the system to be flexible in adapting to a variety of conditions and open-ended situations.

Human rule-following is not quite so mechanistic and determinate. Its inherent indeterminacy affects both the rule-following performance and the way in which a person normatively self-evaluates that performance. For human beings this is done in two contexts:

1. in relation to the variety of natural situations (which, in themselves, favor a high level of flexibility of response rather than specifiable stereotypy of reactions).
2. in the light of discursive interaction and judgments of others on one's performance.

This is quite unlike a formal system in which all that is required is that a determinable next step is taken after each state is produced. The resulting state might be compared with the goal state according to some comparator function and then a further move made to bring the state of the system closer to its goal, but this is still not an evaluation in the rich human sense that we associate with discourse. It is crucial to the system that the various states to be compared and the procedures to be performed are clearly and unambiguously structured in terms of their component data points and that it functions with mechanical regularity. This is the situation that, as we have suggested, is doubly defeated by human rule-following, its contexts and implicit norms.

Beyond the indeterminacy of input and the indeterminacy of goal state that is a feature of human action but not of the model, there is a further problem with this formal state-transformation view as a metaphorical grammar of discursive activity. It fails to predict human performance in the face of a multiplicity of inconclusive inputs and possible combinations that arise from an ecological field of cognition. The problem is that a state-scanning system that looks at the possibilities arising from a multiple or complex set of inputs can rapidly get into a "combinatorial explosion" because there are just too many ways it could go depending on the way the various inputs are treated. This is accentuated when even further inconclusive information is added to the situation. However, human beings do better and not worse when such contextual factors are added (even if they are indefinite in their implications).

The final point that has shifted a number of theorists away from the attempt to construct formal theories of cognition is the existence of what we could call proximity effects in cognitive function. This refers to the fact that stimuli that are corrupted, incomplete, or cognitively proximate to a canonical or preferred stimulus will be treated as if they partially fulfill the requirements for the latter. This is hard to explain if the system is geared to recognize prespecified data points that go to make up a complex but uniquely determinate state. The models that deal best with them are connectionist or neural network models.

Neural Networks

Neural network models have two properties of interest in the present account. First, their structure is reminiscent of brain architecture (as is evident in their name). Second, they seem to be made for a discursive or post-Wittgensteinian account of thought and meaning. This second point will become evident as we discuss how connectionist systems work. The question of the direction of their interpretation, to discourse grammars or to brain processes, is thus inherent in their very name!

At first reading they sound very much as if they are, as their name suggests, abstract representations of brain processes. They have an architecture that accepts parallel inputs from different parts of the sensory domain of the organism. The inputs then set up patterns of excitation in higher levels of the system. The patterns of excitation depend on the preferred configurations to which the system is attuned. We can illustrate these features in a diagram (see Figure 5.1).

The primary inputs (level 1 in the system) feed to secondary units between which there are various relationships of mutual excitation and inhibition. Then there is a third level for detecting three-letter English words. We see that the simply oriented lines in various positions of the first level are used to excite nodes corresponding to letters at the second level. The third level gathers letters into sets of three according to nodes that correspond to English words. Now the system allows for interactions between higher and lower levels so that ambiguous or incomplete stimuli at the first level can be compensated for. We see this in the example shown where the F node has an inconclusive pattern of primary-level input but is favored over the E unit because FIT is a word whereas EIT is not.

Connectionist systems also allow for the growth of patterns of connection according to the relationships prevailing in the domain of activity. There is no need for the deeper or higher level systems to have any predetermined content although they may well have certain prefigured types of stimulus groupings to "aim" at (such as a constant although shifting configuration of stimuli as might arise from a moving object). Thus it is possible for the system to have some inbuilt preferences, for instance, for the human face or the direction of human gaze (Trevarthen, 1992) but also to build up

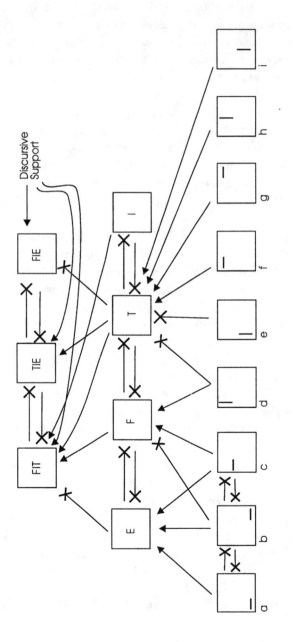

Figure 5.1. A Simple Network

NOTE: At each level, the nodes inhibit one another. Only a selection of excitatory → and inhibitory —× connections are shown. Adding the excitatory inputs should result in the node pattern arising out of the input patterns. Thus f, g, h, and i make the pattern T.

patterns of stimulus linkage that reflect what happens in the environment. This is the kind of flexible adaptation that can exploit the possibilities of a discourse and the significations it offers.

The basic influence on the shape of stimulus usage and the structuring of behavior is the law of effect. This is Thorndike's principle:

> When a modifiable connection between a situation and a response is made and is accompanied or followed by a satisfying state of affairs, that connection's strength is increased: When made and accompanied or followed by an annoying state of affairs, its strength is decreased. (Thorndike, 1913, p. 4)

To see how one might explain this in a connectionist network, we need only observe that the network allows for collateral inputs selectively to favor certain patterns of excitation rather than others depending on factors extrinsic to the stimuli themselves. This might figure in cognitive shaping through the effect of correlative inputs, acting perhaps on the basis of biological relevance, to strengthen or weaken successful groupings and uses of information. On this basis, a person might adopt patterns of connectivity and information use that reflect individual history and his or her interaction with biologically important features of the world. But we should recall that the most relevant biological variable for most developed mammalian species (and particularly for human beings) is the relatedness between different individuals in mutual cooperative activity (Butterworth, 1993). This places great weight on communication and the signs used in communication in the shaping of cognitive structure. Network systems can help to suggest how signs and markers of discursive activity might contribute to cognitive activities as performed with systems of signs, without the system being totally organized around "language in the head." As our account has unfolded, the subject of the model has drifted from seeming to be a representation of the structure of the brain or nervous system, to an expression of the grammar of a complex discursive practice.

Consider Figure 5.2 as to how teaching stimuli might structure an ambiguous domain of information. We can see this in the figure, where we have sketched a simple informational domain with axes a to e and 1 to 5 so that there are 25 potential data points. We have then used this to show how a "marker," arbitrarily connected with a stimulus, may play a role in cognitive activity. This is required because some patterns are very difficult to learn. For instance, the first task—(i) in Figure 5.2—involves the detection of a horizontal line. This is difficult because, if one takes any data point (e.g., $c4$), then it is four times more likely for $c4$ to be OFF than ON during a favored presentation. Thus, as far as the system is concerned, the probability of $c4$ being part of a favored pattern is much lower than the probability of *not-c4* being included.

This problem can be solved by providing the system with a "teaching input" or "cue" to correct responding as in task ii. Here the system has an easy discrimination task because the "cue" ($a1$, $b1$, $c1$, $d1$, $e1 = I1$) is constant in every favored presentation.

However, the neural network not only registers the excitation pattern evoked by the "cue"—$I1$—but also develops a tendency to accept the total pattern ($I1$ + line) as a favored input. Now, when the previously elusive horizontal line pattern is given on its own, it will be regarded as a degraded or incomplete form of the total pattern ($I1$ + line) and be thus responded to. The line can then become a complex stimulus that can be maintained by an appropriate set of contingencies and is therefore recognized where, unaided by the "cue," it would not have been.

Once the line is regarded by the system as a favored pattern, the cue supporting it, $I1$, can be eliminated and the pattern recognition maintained as in Figure 5.2 (iii). In this way, the cue functions as an aid to adaptive discrimination but remains essentially detachable from the object or feature (here the horizontal line) that it has "taught" the system to detect. But when we pursue the analogy between the arbitrary cue, $I1$, and a linguistic term, it appears that the fate of the "cue" may not merely be to fade from the scene after it has successfully linked a certain range of responses to a set of environmental conditions.

```
        1 2 3 4 5
      a . . . . .
      b . . . . .
      c . . . . .        }  the basic domain of information
      d . . . . .
      e . . . . .
```

(i)   the task - discriminate a horizontal line

```
  * * * * *      - - - - -      - - - - -      - - - - -       - - - - -
  - - - - -      * * * * *      - - - - -      - - - - -       - - - - -
  - - - - -      - - - - -      * * * * *      - - - - -       - - - - -
  - - - - -      - - - - -      - - - - -      * * * * *       - - - - -
  - - - - -      - - - - -      - - - - -      - - - - -       * * * * *
p[c4] = 0.2,  p[~c4] = 0.8
```

(ii) task - discriminate line with cue

```
  * * * * *      * - - - -      * - - - -      * - - - -       * - - - -
  * - - - -      * * * * *      * - - - -      * - - - -       * - - - -
  * - - - -      * - - - -      * * * * *      * - - - -       * - - - -
  * - - - -      * - - - -      * - - - -      * * * * *       * - - - -
  * - - - -      * - - - -      * - - - -      * - - - -       * * * * *
p[a1,b1,c1,d1,e1] = 1.0  therefore call this the Invariant  (= I')
```

(iii) task - maintain discrimination without cue

```
  * * * * *      - - - - -      - - - - -      - - - - -       - - - - -
  - - - - -      * * * * *      - - - - -      - - - - -       - - - - -
  - - - - -      - - - - -      * * * * *      - - - - -       - - - - -
  - - - - -      - - - - -      - - - - -      * * * * *       - - - - -
  - - - - -      - - - - -      - - - - -      - - - - -       * * * * *
```

In (iii), p values no longer relevant because recognition is
adaptively maintained.
                           UNLESS
(iv)   I' is also a cue for another domain

```
  1 2 3 4 5
v - - - - -                  * * * - -      * - - - -       * - - - -
w - - - - -                  * - - * -      * * * - -       * - - - -
x - - - - -    so that       * - - - *      * - - * -       * * * - -
y - - - - -                  * - - - -      * - - - *       * - - * -
z - - - - -                  * - - - -      * - - - -       * - - - *
```

Thus I' helps to bring about the connection:
```
                                             * * *
      * * * * *      <-------->                 *

                                                 *
```

Figure 5.2. The Use of a Teaching or Cue Stimulus

A linguistic term such as a word may link to more than one set of conditions. For instance, the word *handle* is used as a noun to denote certain objects, as a verb to indicate a certain type of activity, and has obvious lexical relations to the term *hand*. The word therefore helps to secure the link between the activity and the objects involved in that activity (this could properly be called an internal link). It also serves as a focus and marker for a whole repertoire or multiplicity of articulated terms and activities (Wittgenstein, 1975, sec. 32) that contribute to or supplement the use of the human hand. The analogy is picked up in task iv, where $I1$ functions as a cue for another domain of sensitivity (i.e., it is simultaneously detected both by $[a1, b1, c1, d1, e1]$ and by $[v1, w1, x1, y1, z1]$). $I1$'s co-occurrence in these two different processing domains means that a connection is set up between the configuration registered in the first domain (a horizontal line) and that in the second (the crooked line). The cue therefore serves here both a detection-aiding function and a connection-forming function for patterns that are subtle within the informational array and that may never have been detected, let alone connected, without it. In this way cues can set up categories of stimuli (horizontal lines, crooked lines) and links between stimuli fulfilling the different categorical types.

We can plausibly regard meanings as marked by arbitrary or conventional symbols that are used within human discourse to structure different activities. In this view, meanings (the senses— as Frege (1973) understood this notion—of linguistic terms) are groupings and orderings of stimulus patterns and connections between stimulus patterns. Just such a view is suggested by Luria's characterization of a word as a "complex multidimensional matrix of different cues and connections" (p. 306). Neural network theory enables us to hazard a guess as to how meanings, construed in this way, could shape or influence the microprocessing structure of the brain by setting up nodes or configurations of sensitivities to patterns of information and then forming connections between those functional nodes.

At this point we can briefly review the features of our neuro-cognitive sketch that illuminate the way that meanings figure in cognition.

1. The symbol or meaning-marker picks out for the cognitive subject the category or basis of unity between different presented arrays of stimuli.
2. The cue is detachable from the category and may have no "natural" connection with it.
3. The cue is facilitatory for different connections so that the system of interconnected processing pathways that results can be relatively holistic.
4. Cues can link the detection of stimuli by different subjects so that they converge upon the same range of items or features as instances of a given type.
5. Cues can impose constraints on inclusion of stimulus presentations where the "uncued" input may be incompletely distinguished due to considerable informational overlap between acceptable inputs.

The central role of words in this process implies that the attempt to reduce human representation to a set of individualistic, biologically understood transactions between organisms and physical features of their environment are misconceived. It suggests that instead of construing the "rules" that structure human cognition as analyzable in terms of reactions to distal objects or proximal stimulus patterns by nonsocial animals (Millikan, 1990, p. 331), we should look at human rule-following in terms more conducive to recognizing the social dimension of human behavior.

A Rapprochement Between Thought and Cognition

The possibility of a link between this contemporary work in cognitive science and discursive psychology emerges when we recall that the idea of mental content or meaning (as a way of theorizing about discourse) is tied to rules and rule-following. The convergences and differences between two philosophers serve to sharpen the issue between individualism and social engagement as the proper framework within which to understand the mind.

Kant's model of the mind is an inner realm of rationally ordered operations using concepts in accordance with the laws of reason. He characterizes concepts as "predicates of possible judgments" (Kant, 1929 [1789], p. B94) that rest on "functions of unity among our representations" (pp. B93-B94). He argues that in judgments we "subsume" objects or phenomena (out there) under rules (in the inner realm). These "rules of the understanding" give specifications of what counts as falling under this or that concept. A person uses the faculty of judgment to relate these (normative) schemata to actual (or imaginary) objects. Kant concentrates on cognitive processes of a type most appropriate to generate spatiotemporal schemata with mathematical properties and he neglects common predicates like *red, lumpy,* or *dog.* Schematism, for Kant, is the process whereby a thinker achieves specifications of what count as instances of a given concept. The generation of a schema by a cognitive subject involves a "rule of synthesis in the imagination" that provides "an image for a concept" (p. B180).

Kant does not discuss how a person comes to be equipped with and uses this logico-mathematically structured system (whose rules determine which things are to count as of this or that type). However, Kant's notion that there is a schema or cognitive specification that structures our perception of objects and articulates it within a broader framework of knowledge and practical reasoning is echoed in recent cognitive psychology.

We have noted that Neisser (1976) uses the idea of a schema to denote the complex of active exploratory skills that directs and serves to organize the information gathered from the interaction between a person as cognitive subject and the world. The schema is "internal to the perceiver, modifiable by experience, and somehow specific to what is being perceived" (p. 54). But although the schema is here conceived as internal to the perceiver, Neisser is open to the possibility that social influences and linguistic interaction (which we have identified as being at the heart of meaningful activity) are an intrinsic part of the development of schemata. He remarks that the objects of perception "belong coherently to a larger context, possess an identity that transcends their simple physical properties" (Neisser, 1976, p. 71). This implicit or suggested social connection suggests that a fruitful strand of psychological theory could be initiated by pursuing the relation between the meanings that underpin cognitive schemata and the social determinants of those meanings.

Kant held that the "outer" world of material things and causal processes and the "inner" world of thoughts and feelings, as they are experienced by human beings, are jointly produced from a flux of undifferentiated sensations. He thought that the production of an experienced world and a mental realm of thought is achieved by synthesis according to rule.

A discursive analysis of concepts can pick up Kant's notion of *synthesis* and expand it in two ways.

1. Anything a person experiences must be the focus of cognitive skills that suffice to bring out those features adequate to ground a certain signification, that is, to reveal a certain meaning.
2. The information derived from a situation must be judged to be in accordance with the norms that govern the use of a concept or conception. Both of these aspects of cognitive activity have to do with the ability of human beings to discover in particular cases instances of general conceptual types.

The first aspect is a skilled data assembly or sorting function, seeing a pattern of colors as an animal, and the second involves rule-governed instance-grouping, seeing that animal as a giraffe.

Frege, who has inspired much contemporary theory on thought and its contents, required that an account of meaning should not be individualistic or solipsistic (Frege, 1977, p. 17). This suggests that we ought to move away from Kant's focus on the individual rational subject and look to a broader framework to understand meaning and rule-following. Wittgenstein's discussion of rules does just this and provides, as we have noted, the departure point for discursive psychology.

Wittgenstein can be read as arguing that for a sign to have a meaning is for it to have a rule-governed use. Rules, as we have noted, are not happily thought of as dispositional entities that causally produce certain states or behavior in a specific range of conditions. Human rules incorporate reasons or justifications (in terms of a discourse and the dynamics of that discourse) for organizing one's current behavior according to particular significations. The social and cultural aspects of such rule-following and Wittgenstein's insistence that one cannot follow (in principle) private rules imply that discursive readings of his position are more than plausible. Following a rule is achieved by mastering a public practice the norms of which are socially enforced and stabilized by reference to public exemplars and, in principle, independent of one's own internal functioning. In fact, human rule-followers not only follow rules but conceive of themselves as under discursive constraints. This is evident in the recognition that one can neither determine, unilaterally and for oneself, what counts as an instance of a concept, say, "cat," nor what is implicit in classifying a thing as instantiating that concept. These two aspects of the grasp of a concept, respectively, forge links between the concept and the world (application) and the concept and other concepts (cognitive role). Both aspects of a concept (the use of a word or sign) are rule-governed and, in adapting to the constraints imposed by the relevant rules, a person implicitly recognizes a distinction between what seems right to them and what it *is right* to do. For this reason, people must adopt normative attitudes to their own responses when they aim at using a word or sign to structure their mental activity.

There is a natural link between these philosophical considerations about thought and meaning and the examples of cognitive microprocessing we have described. A symbol can be used as a cue that enables one to detect a point of significance in the environment where that point is picked out by the practices legitimated in one's social context. So the word *cat,* as used in such a remark as "Look at the cat!" enables a person to pick out something from their surroundings. That symbol embodies a canonical or normatively defined set of conditions on the basis of criteria (Baker, 1974), affordances (Gibson, 1979), including "social affordances" (McArthur & Baron, 1983), family resemblances, or whatever instantiates the concept in question. It can also figure in different areas of activity and so forge links between different sets of conditions that articulate the individual's behavior (Wittgenstein, 1975, sec. 32). Thus the word *cat* can figure in an instruction such as "Put the cat's saucer outside the back door" and so on. These two aspects of the function of cues or symbols are plausibly explained on the basis of the simple neural network models used above and, as we have noted, correspond, respectively, to the application of a word to experience and to the cognitive role of a concept or semantic element in the management of practical activities. The neural network model is a metaphor for a discursive grammar. These latter features of concept (word or sign) use are under discursive control; we think according to norms that pervade our discursive setting.

Thus the influences shaping individual cognition and the thoughts framed by people are social and interpersonal. They suggest that structuration or the formative influence of discourse on individual psychology is, at heart, a process that happens to persons as beings in relation, not as Cartesian subjects (self-contained, individualistic, cognitive systems apt for study according to the canons of methodological solipsism). The relational aspects of semantic training also go some way toward explaining an interesting fact disclosed by recent cognitive research in personality: "Our ways of knowing the world are intrinsically bound up with our ways of feeling" (Singer and Kolligian, 1987, p. 548). One would expect that emotive or conative influences such as those that pervade interpersonal relations would be important in knowing if knowing itself was based on techniques mastered in just such relationships.

A further implication of this view of semantic (i.e., conceptual or contentful) psychological activity is that psychological properties are not straightforwardly causal. People conform or do not conform to certain rule-governed practices based on relatively holistic personal relations to those who attempt to impart semantic rules. As represented in the neural network model (metaphor), the (relative) holism is accomplished by allowing multiple interactions between subsystems responsive to different domains of stimuli and patterns of presentation. This holism means that patterns of excitation in diverse parts of the system may or may not develop informationally effective links to events in other parts. Thus different information processing subsystems faced with a given set of conditions may work in very different ways depending on collateral activity in other (perhaps motivational) centers of the total system within which they operate. Thus one might expect that cognitive operations—while tied to publicly determined semantic components and therefore accessible intersubjectively on the basis of shared norms—would exhibit some individualism in their detailed psychological roles or contents (Frege, 1977, p. 10). One could say that normalized discursive roles are compatible with varying degrees of individualistic use and association. We shall return to these suggestive hints when we discuss subjectivity, action, and personality.

We should, at this point, return to the dual semantics of the neural network model. As we have suggested, it does allow us to construct a picture of what might be going on (unobservably, at a neural level) when people engage in discourse. It also allows us to understand the informal aspects of cognition in terms of a theoretical model of cognition. And it might yet be that the neural network models, whose justification at present must come from their role for representing grammars, could be supported in literal "neural" interpretation, just as the molecular model of gas is, on the one hand, interpretable as a representation of the laws of the behavior of samples of gas and, on the other, as a "picture" of the behavior of swarms of molecules.

Conclusion

It seems mistaken to try to explain human thought in terms of formal syllogisms and inferences, and a calculus of predetermined moves between propositions. Human thought is informal and highly sensitive to discursive context with all its real-world richness and relational structure. In its place we have put a multitude of practical uses of words and other signs as the essence of thought. In developing "cognitive" models of the dynamics of these practices, we picture cognitive systems that can cope with the complexity and variety of real-world experience and are not bound by rigid specifications of information. Such systems are appropriate to carry the meanings arising in discourse into the techniques used to structure experience and solve the problems posed in an inherently unstructured environment.

We shall now turn to the way in which we might conceptualize the relationship between this discourse-based approach and the study of brain function, implicit in the essential ambiguity (or dual semantics) at the core of cognitive model making. A cognitive model that is an adequate representation of the rules of discursive activity should also be capable of being interpreted as an abstract representation of the brain processes through which the activity is implemented.

❖ 6 ❖

Discourse and the Brain

The brain is structured like a language.
not-Lacan

This survey of the discursive turn in psychology is, in part, an attempt to resurrect the full Aristotelian conception of a human being as a rational, social animal. According to this conception we need not only the idea that human beings are active agents undertaking various projects in accordance with local conventions of propriety and correctness but also an understanding of how discourse shapes the brain. Discursive contexts, the activities in which we engage in them, and the skills we acquire to accomplish these activities must somehow produce the neurological substrate of skilled action that is modeled by the cognitive metaphors such as we sketched in the last chapter. Some writers have already attempted to point in this direction; Manicas (1986) remarks that "some higher-level processes appear to penetrate in a causal way at lower levels" (p. 74). He suggests that we might, for instance, try to integrate diverse modes of psychological explanations so as to accommodate social, cultural, and structural influences as well as more conventionally understood stimulus/ input/energy transfer models of human cognition. He even suggests that "there is always the possibility that neurobiological mechanisms are themselves alterable as a consequence of different social environments" (Manicas, 1986, p. 74). We will argue that this conjecture has received considerable support from recent cognitive neuroscience. In fact, if we seriously believe in a broadly Aristotelian theory of mind—that in performing discursive, symbolic activities, the mindful agent makes use of the properties of brain mechanisms—there seems no alternative but to assert that social influences shape brain function. The brain, for any individual human being, is the repository of meanings in that it serves as the physical medium in which mental content is realized and plays a part in the discursive activities of individuals (Gillett, 1992a). In this respect it is no different than the neuromuscular system, which is "shaped" by learning to play tennis and is thereby rendered available as the appropriate instrument for the minded agent to play a match with.

At this point in our discussion we must, perforce, launch upon a discourse based on mentalistic metaphors, whose topic is the structure of and processes in a thoroughly nonmentalistic entity, the human brain and nervous system. To help the reader "keep the books," we shall use single quotes to highlight those expressions that are drawn from the mentalistically organized models of brain functioning that we discussed briefly in the previous chapter. We must warn, too, that the double reference of models of cognition has led to a subtle extension of the meaning of that very term. The word *cognition* has come to be the generic term for all kinds of higher level activities, many of which could not reasonably be identified as "thought."

Throughout life, the brain stores 'experience in terms of the meanings' that have structured that experience and the responses made by the individual to aspects of the events experienced. We have argued that the meanings used to structure the responses of an individual draw on rules that have been shaped in human discourse. This implies there must be a deep relation between the language that a community speaks and the categorizations or significations that members of that community use to unify stimulus presentations and group them into meaningful patterns. In this way, interpersonal rules and the terms they govern can be thought of as producing the articulation (complex patterns of interconnectedness) in human behavior that ultimately explains our multiplicity of responses to things around us. In fact, the role of words in forming and refining our thoughts is, as we have noted, becoming increasingly clear from theoretical, clinical, and experimental work in cognitive psychology (Karmiloff-Smith, 1979; Luria, 1973; Vygotsky, 1962).

We have already discussed the fact that the way that words operate to fulfill their cognitive role and to organize brain function can be expressed in models whose fruitful ambiguity permits the double interpretation that is characteristic of the great models used in the physical sciences. Neural network theory and practice has just the same fruitful duality of interpretation as does the kinetic theory of gases. The neurological terminology is metaphorical in relation to the employment of the model as a grammar of the relevant discourses, and literal (or close to it) in relation to the employment of the model as an abstract representation of brain processes.

The relationship of the condition of the brain to conscious experience is a fascinating topic. The basic discoveries were made in a classic series of studies by Wilder Penfield.

Twenty-six years ago I was operating on a woman under local anaesthesia in the Royal Victoria Hospital and was applying to different points on the temporal lobe of her brain a stimulating electrode. She (E.W.) told me suddenly that she seemed to be living over again a previous experience. She seemed to see herself giving birth to her baby girl. That happened years before, and meanwhile the girl had grown up. The mother was now lying on the operating table in my operating room, hoping that I could cure her attacks of focal epilepsy.

This, I thought, was a strange moment for her to talk of that previous experience, but then, I reflected, women were unpredictable, and it was never intended that men should understand them completely. Nevertheless, I noted the fact that it was while my stimulating electrode was applied to the left temporal lobe that this woman had this unrelated and vivid recollection. That was in 1931. (Penfield, 1958, p. 52)

Penfield's discursive commitments, particularly in relation to one area of interpersonal relationships, are quaintly evident in his text. He went on to record a number of observations of such phenomena in different patients (numbering nearly 1,000), in each of which the experience was as if the person was recalling an actual incident from his or her past. Penfield came to the following conclusion:

There is, hidden away in the brain, a record of the stream of consciousness. It seems to hold the detail of that stream as laid down during each man's waking conscious hours. Contained in this record are all those things of which the individual was once aware—such detail as a man might hope to remember for a few seconds or minutes afterward but which are largely lost to voluntary recall after that time. The things that he ignored are absent from that record. (Penfield, 1958, p. 56)

It is clear that Penfield's assertions outstrip his evidence by a considerable margin but his conclusion highlights the incontrovertible fact that the brain is plastic in the face of experience. It develops the processing structure required to underpin the discursive skills evident in perception, action, and problem solving and also holds some kind of 'record of past experience' that can be used to make available the recall of autobiographical episodes. As a result of these properties of the brain, a person is provided with a narrative resource that is built out of their own individual history, much as the arrangement of the iron particles on a magnetic tape may hold the 'record' of a conversation. The structure of this 'record' and the skills that enable the subject to make use of it are a function of discourse but the brain is the substrate for the requisite mental activity. Therefore we need to explore the resonances between our knowledge of brain function and that of conscious, discursive activity. In so doing we will try to make good Luria's claim concerning the role of discourse in the organization of cerebral activity.

> The chief distinguishing feature of the regulation of human conscious activity is that this regulation takes place with the close participation of *speech*. Whereas the relatively elementary forms of regulation of organic processes and even of the simplest forms of behavior can take place without the aid of speech, *higher mental processes are formed and take place on the basis of speech activity*. (Luria, 1973, pp. 93-94)

We shall begin our investigation of this claim by considering Luria's own account of neuropsychology.

Luria

Luria has consistently taken the view that language pervades psychological functions. He, like Allport in relation to cognition, rejects the idea that there is a direct relationship between recognizable mental abilities such as perception, memory, and so on and localized cerebral processes (Luria, 1973, p. 42). He observes that there are a plenitude of descending influences from higher to lower levels of brain function. This is consistent with the essential thrust of his account, namely, that meaningful or language-related activity organizes cerebral processing.

The most common approach to determining how the structure of cognition is realized in brain function is to conduct various tests in which patients with neurological damage respond to tasks set by an investigator. The investigator attempts to construct tasks that explore different aspects of cognitive function. For instance, the task might involve matching individual pictures to the components of a complex picture of overlapping objects and then independently asking the patient to identify individual component pictures by their name or use (McCarthy and Warrington, 1990, p. 30). If someone were able to do the first but not the second, that would suggest that the brain lesion involved had no effect on complex shape discrimination but impaired the appreciation of the meaning or function of pictured objects. By using batteries of such tests one can decide with a great deal of precision on the cognitive capacities that "keep company" in the brain. These in turn are assumed to tell us something about the development of and connections between different 'cognitive functions.'

In discussing perception, Luria is keen to point out that the greatly expanded processing centers in the parietal areas of the human cortex are responsible for multimodal integration of stimuli so as to assemble a package of activity sensitive to the presence of objects of a certain type as they are encountered in the real world. These areas combine input through different sensory systems and, in humans, the higher cortical zones assume the dominant role in organizing these integrative and object specification functions. This brings him to a claim about cerebral dominance.

> The left (dominant) hemisphere (in right-handers) begins to play an essential role not only in the cerebral organization of speech but also in the *cerebral organization of all higher forms of cognitive activity connected with speech*—perception organized into logical schemes, active verbal memory, logical thought—whereas the right (non-dominant) hemisphere either begins to play a subordinate role in the cerebral organization of these processes or plays no part whatsoever in their course. (Luria, 1973, p. 78)

When we add the dominance (in human beings) of left-hemisphere function to the general control exerted by the frontal lobes, which Luria consistently notes as being the locus of cerebral realization of social and speech-based organization, the thesis that meaningful or discursive activity is central in human behavior, derived from the naturalistic study of human life, not surprisingly, has its counterpart in a thesis about the hierarchical organization of the physical brain itself.

According to Luria, the frontal lobes regulate attention and activation and therefore take part in perception (Luria, 1973,

p. 217) and the focusing of cognitive abilities. They are what
we are putting to use in forward planning of intentional activity
(Luria, 1973, p. 198). He observes that damage to the frontal lobes
affects the ability of a person to perform the complex, flexible,
and adaptive regulation of conscious activity and leads to impul-
sive and stereotyped behavior that lacks long-term stability. This
loss of the ability to regulate one's activities by well-formed and
articulated intentions is also evident in the fact that patients lose
"the ability to check their results in complex tasks" (Luria, 1973,
p. 210). The intellectual or problem-solving abilities of patients
with damage to the frontal lobes are also disturbed.

> The patient either substitutes a series of impulsive, fragmentary guesses
> for true intellectual activity, or reproduces inert stereotypes instead of
> the adequate and adaptable programme of the intellectual act. (Luria,
> 1973, p. 212)

Luria's view shines through his writings about neuropsychological function. He regards discursive or speech-based activity as the
key to understanding brain function. But we should not be misled
by this summary of his views. He is not making the simplistic claim
that there is a "language of thought" (Fodor, 1975) or the virtually
unintelligible claim that the propositional calculus is built into the
architecture of the brain. He regards speech, and therefore language-
as-realized-in-human-communication, as an organized form of conscious activity rather than as a calculus or computational structure
making use of definable components and specifications of input.
We could gloss his whole approach as founded on the view that
discourse and usage, particularly of the tools made available in
natural language, penetrate deep into the organizational structure
of the brain, in the sense that in the course of the acquisition of
all sorts of discursive and manual skills brain structure is transformed to provide the machinery that an active human agent puts
to work in exercising those skills in a multiplicity of tasks of everyday life.

Contemporary Neuropsychological Data

Many contemporary neuropsychologists would not accept Luria's claim that the influence of speech and language are central in the genesis of cerebral organization. They argue, on the basis of the apparent dissociability of cognitive functions, that many cognitive tasks, such as visual perception of complex figures, can proceed concurrently with profound impairment of comprehension of verbal material (McCarthy and Warrington, 1990). To think that such evidence counts against the Luria-Vygotsky thesis betrays a profound misunderstanding of their view. Allport, in particular, is keen to demonstrate that language and thought are separable in our understanding of the cognitive effects of various types of brain damage. He contends, based on a series of studies, that

> at least some forms of human reasoning can survive, and at a level of competence that evinces . . . a high level of relative intelligence, even when the cerebral machinery necessary for the generation and the comprehension of natural language has been substantially destroyed. (Allport, 1983, p. 68)

To be fair, Allport never uses this evidence against Luria. It is evident that it does not hit the mark in respect to Luria's theory. Luria is not arguing that explicit 'speech' mechanisms (of the type that generate and allow current comprehension of speech) are intrinsic to the exercise of all 'intellectual faculties.' He claims that the organizing power of speech as a complex form of communicative activity influences the way that the brain sets up its 'information processing' functions, which then can be employed upon tasks that may be quite remote from the discursive activities that were involved in their creation. The Luria-Vygotsky claim is a principle of neuropsychological development.

McCarthy and Warrington (1990) have summarized a vast amount of material from contemporary 'cognitive' neuropsychology. They begin their survey by discussing perception. They note that there are three stages of visual perception discriminable on the basis of the differential effect of brain lesions. The first stage involves purely visual analysis of the structure of the pattern of stimulation. The next involves a structural, again visual, specification of the object, and the third involves its meaning or 'functional significance' without which "knowledge of an object cannot be said to be fully established" (McCarthy and Warrington, 1990, p. 51). This is the level of appreciation of an object that is intrinsically connected to the part it plays in the life of the subject. This is, of course, the context within which discursive meaning takes shape and, as we have often remarked, it is pervaded by signs and rules that define the techniques we share as members of communicating groups.

A further set of interesting observations concerns the dissociability of two different ways of responding to complex presentations. The processing of information from human faces seems to be separable into the perceptual processing of familiar faces on the one hand and the representation of familiar faces on the other. This is meat and drink to a discursive analysis in which human faces (or indeed objects of other classes) have a vastly different significance in discourse depending on their familiarity. Recall Wittgenstein's question: "How do I know that this is a picture of *him*?" Some human faces have the significance <a person known to me> and others merely <a face with a certain appearance>. There is a world of difference between these two significations in terms of the relationships that define my attitudes toward, projects concerning, and intentions with regard to the person with that face and that would be expected to be reflected in the way the brain deals with the 'information' establishing a pattern as having 'one or the other content.' However, if we regard human 'information processing' without reference to the discursive context in which I locate myself and the engagement between myself and others, these differences are not apparent.

Neuropsychologists test voluntary motor activity by using tasks such as bimanual coordination, copying single movements and sequences of movement, making familiar gestures, using real objects, and pantomiming the use of objects. There is a consistent tendency for left-hemisphere lesions to produce greater impairment in these tasks. Given Luria's insistence that complex planned movements and action patterns are established with the aid of speech, this finding is not unexpected. This is entirely consistent with the general view that "disorders of voluntary movement could be explained in terms of deficits in conceptualisation or in linking concepts with sensory motor associations" (attributed to Leipmann, 1905, by McCarthy and Warrington, 1990). But this does not imply that there is explicit verbal mediation of the voluntary activity, only that the same practiced, discursively informed, and regulated skills that underlie language use (and therefore meaning) are generally important in the structure of the management of any human behavior. It is plausible that the left hemisphere of the brain assumes dominance over the mechanisms we use in the direction of our behavior because of the pervasive role of speech in the contexts where voluntary activity is developed and refined.

A very interesting finding in the cerebral organization of the neural mechanisms with which we implement word comprehension and word finding is that both of these aspects of the use of language are susceptible to "category-specific deficits." This has been a recurrent theme of work on cognitive disorders by Warrington and McCarthy and it suggests that semantically ordered systems of language processing skills produce a corresponding fundamental feature of neuro-'cognitive' architecture. For instance, the partial preservation of understanding of words tends to reflect semantic approximation to the correct response rather than morphemic, phonemic, or syntactic approximation. This is what one would expect if the neural machinery available to someone for the performance of the task was a (partially damaged) semantically structured neural network system that was 'doing its best' to channel activation into a pathway that fit the stimulus. If one makes the discursive turn, then the fundamental influences on the brain mechanisms that a person uses to implement cognitive tasks would have just this meaningful character. Subjects would approximate according to the usages and real-life context relations

between presented items of information and not on other artificially constructed parameters.

A last piece of neuropsychological data relevant to the current
project arises in memory research. Short-term memory has a measurable capacity but this capacity can be dramatically changed if the
meaningful shape of the data is changed. This has been most clearly
observed when a patient is tested on lists of words and sentences
and the relative performances assessed (Saffran and Marin, 1975).
The patient could remember a greater number of words as a meaningful sentence than as an unconnected list. What is more, the
sentences produced in error "were a close approximation to the
target sentence and retained its gist" (McCarthy and Warrington,
1990, p. 277). We must assume that the mechanism by which short-
term memory tasks are accomplished is affected by the meaningfulness to the subject of the information presented for processing.

We might therefore conclude that there is, as Luria suggests,
extensive and thoroughgoing penetration of the meaningful into
the organization of brain function. This allows us to reinterpret
some contentious evidence on so-called split-brain patients.

Split-Brain Findings

Roger Sperry, a neuropsychologist, did extensive work in the
1950s and 1960s on patients who had had the great cerebral com-
missure (the band of fibers connecting the two sides of the brain)
split to try to control epilepsy. He found that, even though such
patients could organize their day-by-day activity perfectly adequately, they could be shown to have discontinuities in their cognitive performance on tests that successfully isolated one or the
other hemisphere in terms of the 'information' presented to it. If,
for instance, the patient was told to look at a spot on a screen and
then a picture of a pipe was flashed into the right visual field, the
right hand (controlled by the left hemisphere) could pick out a
pipe as the object shown on the screen but the left hand could not
(Sperry, 1965). Sperry concluded from this and other findings that

there were two streams of consciousness created by the separation of the hemispheres. Some of those who have commented on his findings would go so far as to say that there are two minds in such people. But Sperry himself had noted that the patients had an uncanny ability to correct their mistakes when the 'ignorant' hemisphere guessed wrongly. Often a patient would frown or tut-tut in self-reprimand for an incorrect guess or express commendation if the answer was right. Notice what is happening here: The patient is treating him- or herself as a thinker (one thinker or mind) who has a problem in that they go wrong from time to time. Recall that the performance of the patient in normal contexts is almost indiscernible from that of a normal person. These two observations alone suggest that we should not jump to the conclusion that mental unity is solely a function of a physical connection between two sides of the brain or that hemispheres have minds.

The mind with its stream of consciousness is a function of a person exercising certain discourse-based skills that are synchronically and diachronically integrated to produce an adaptive response to the life situations that person confronts. If the normal underpinning of those skills is disrupted, then it is no wonder that cognitive "cracks" should appear but it is more important to focus on the fact that the person can and does get their act together, mentally speaking, rather than being left "in two minds." Such a person does exhibit certain artificially induced difficulties in situations where we systematically (as part of the study) exclude the use of skills such as scanning the environment by visual search for information and checking on information by using multiple data gathering techniques. This falls far short of having two consciousnesses or identities in the one human body. To make our way in these matters, we must keep our metaphors under very tight reign!

The Brain, Connectionism, and Discourse

Penfield (1958) noted that when he stimulated the same points in the brain he could not rely on his patient having the same experiential images. Stimulation at approximately the same point and close in time to the original stimulation, however, was "apt to reproduce the same experience, beginning at the same moment of time" (p. 58). This is in contrast to stimulation at the same point but delayed, which "is apt to produce an experience that is similar in content or subject" (Penfield, 1958, p. 58). He also notes that "two experiences or strips of time are never activated concurrently" (p. 59). One way to explain these findings is by drawing on the theory of neural networks, with which we can model both the grammar of the discursive phenomenon and the structure of the brain process one would usually use to accomplish it. In a network, similar 'experiences' are recorded or recoverable from the excitation patterns of a particular part of the network. When one pattern of excitation is activated, it inhibits others, and thus the network segment, despite being able to produce different contents, does not confuse them. But, depending on where the network is stimulated, one obtains a specific member of a set of related patterns that have certain things in common.

We have already suggested that it is plausible to suppose that brain networks are structured according to the way 'presented patterns of information' figure in discursive contexts. We have noted the evidence, which suggests that semantic categories or meaningful features are a major determinant in the grouping of 'information' in brain networks. This is what we would expect if cognition reflects the way that objects figure in discursive contexts rather than more theoretical or formal resemblances between them. We seem to be able to get a double dissociation between the semantic appreciation of objects and their more definable geometric properties. This suggests that the meaning of an object to a person is not totally dependent on the construction of a precise specification of the stimulus. In fact, we learn more than this; we learn that the discourse in which objects are abstracted from a complex bundle of impressions making up a situation is different than that in which we classify a thing as being of this or that meaningful type. The brain, it seems, keeps faith with the diversity of skills used by individuals in the real world rather than going "single track" with a complex computational mechanism working in a purely 'information processing' mode. We see a similar phenomenon with the 'processing' of language. The semantic properties of words and sentences seem to survive considerable disruption of their purely syntactic properties. Again, this is what one would expect if the formal analysis of syntax was related to, but not an intrinsic part of, the understanding of discourse. It seems, for instance, that a person can get the general drift of what was being said without having any detailed appreciation of the syntax of an utterance or inscription. This is a predictable feature of the skills involved in discourse when our models are based on the neural network system metaphor, where an approximation to the canonical input may still suffice to produce a coherent response.

The other feature of brain-damaged patients that supports the fruitfulness of using the 'network' model for the interpretation of the discursive activities of such patients is the phenomenon of partial knowledge and partial competence. McCarthy and Warrington (1990) mention a case in which partial semantic knowledge of the type of object to be identified ("No, not another *** household object, I don't recognise those") was the response offered to a cup (p. 55). Luria (1973) records a commonly observed phenomenon in dysphasia that also indicates partial function (p. 140). When one examines the flow of speech from a patient with nominal dysphasia, one often finds that the utterance, though lacking substantive nouns, manages to convey a sense or meaning such that a sympathetic listener can get the drift of what is being said. The same is true of the speech of people with Alzheimer's condition (Sabat and Harré, 1992).

The link between connectionism and discursive psychology in attempting to understand brain function can be summarized by outlining what one of us has called "the holographic analogy" of representation. In a photographic hologram, the object is illuminated by two sources of laser light and the interference between the light waves is then captured on a photographic plate. The resulting image looks nothing like the object even under a transformation (as, for instance, in a "negative" image). But when the

laser light   laser light
the object ──────→ the plate ──────→ the image

                                is like

discourse   discourse
experience ──────→ the brain ──────→ behavior

Figure 6.1. The Holographic Analogy
SOURCE: Gillett (1992b).

plate is itself transilluminated by laser light of the same frequency
as that used to produce the image and a three-dimensional image
is projected, it captures more information than a simple (two-
dimensional) photographic representation. The analogy is pictured
in Figure 6.1.

The present view is that representations of experience are organized in the brain according to the structure and content of the
discourses in which the subject is embedded. When we want to
unlock particular capacities that are realized in the brain, we need
to return the person to something similar to the discursive contexts
in which the relevant meanings and significations were developed
or appreciated. When we do this, the behavior that tends to be
available will comprise responses and structured activity associated with that discourse. These will be understood as we analyze
the orientation of the subject to that context and the multiplicity
of significations intrinsic to it. Our success in adaptation will not
therefore be built on our own biological adaptation to the physical
objects present in a situation but on our cultural and social history
of investing certain things with meaning.

This discursive illumination of situations structures behavior
(which at times, of course, reflects very natural and general human
response types common to many sociocultural contexts). In the

absence of the establishment of interactions (such as test settings) that engage with this discursive structure, we will not learn a great deal about a person's cognitive capacities or discern the potential that remains in a damaged individual. If, however, we do recall and make use of the human context in which that person has developed as a cognizer, then we should learn a great deal about their abilities. This first aspect of our analogy has focused on the medium (laser light or discourse) that gets the information into and out of the representational device (photographic plate or brain). There is, however, another aspect to the analogy.

We are encouraged by the analogy to conceive of the brain as a number of overlapping 'representational' fields each of which is structured by discourse so as to realize some aspect of psychological function. Thus the analogy is more properly to multiple holographic imagery devices focusing on different types of information and its metaphorical counterpart 'information.' Each holographic image is holistic in that any fragment of the plate will reproduce the image but in cruder form than that which would be obtained from the whole plate. When we consider the 'cognitive fields' in the brain, we see an analogous property. A part of the system or area involved in some function performs that function incompletely and in a holistic fashion. Therefore, when the area we use in the naming of objects is damaged, we see some preservation of semantic content for a diversity of subject matters rather than a complete disruption as would occur with a system that worked with fairly rigid and formal lexical operations. We get the sense that the record of the experience is there but it is only partially manifestable until the system finds new ways of doing old and well-practiced tricks. The fact that the tricks are approximated in the interim and then reconstructible out of the neurocognitive remnants of the 'representational field' is powerful evidence for the holism suggested by the analogy. It is, again, exactly what would be expected from a connectionist system working in the flexible way required to adapt to the flux of interpersonal discourse.

Conclusion

Throughout this chapter the animating idea has been that the brain is a custom-made (nonartifactual) instrument that we put to use to accomplish certain tasks, many of which are discursive. We have surveyed the way in which a discursive approach to the analysis of what people do deals with material derived from cognitive neuroscience. The two approaches to psychological investigations are very different and employ vastly different techniques but can be thought of as complementary to one another. Our central, neural network model has the fruitful property of being capable of being treated as an abstract picture of brain structures and processes *and* as a formal model of the grammar (or structure and function) of discourses created by the use of those brain structures. This is a further example of the double analogy of 'cognitive' models that links them so fruitfully to two aspects of the psychophysiological world and so permits them to play a decisive role in mind/brain science. When one asks why a particular behavior has become impaired, specialists in each field go about the investigation in different ways in accordance with each of the readings of the central model. 'Cognitive' neuroscience asks what mechanisms that a normal person would use to accomplish some cognitive function have been damaged. Discursive psychology looks at the areas of discourse and adaptation to discursive contexts that have been affected. These two studies have different foci but are or should both be involved in the study of a complex biological organism whose nature reflects both physical capacity and discursive engagement.

The Discursive Origins
of the Sense of Self

The Aims of Psychological Research

What is it that, as psychologists, we would like to find out about human beings and some animals? We can talk vaguely about the methods of discursive psychology, but what would one actually do if one were trying to do some psychological research from the discursive point of view? How would one start? We are going to illustrate the practice of discursive psychology with several examples. In the doing of psychological research, we shall see, particularly, the moment at which anthropology enters into studies. There are really two main aims in psychological research, according to the discursive point of view.

1. One wants to find out what resources people have to accomplish their plans, projects, and intentions. What repertoire of concepts do they have available as usable sign systems, and what are their capacities for the uses of words and other signs? A term has recently been introduced for their repertoire (Stearns and Stearns, 1988). The resources people have available in some roughly delineated, cultural system have been called an ". . . -ology." So an "emotionology" is a representation of the linguistic and other discursive resources people have available for describing emotional phenomena. If we follow the pattern of "emotionology," we might also investigate a "self-and-person-ology," the result of the study of the resources people have for identifying and describing selves and persons in a specific culture, and so on.

2. These resources are put to work in the coordinated actions of the episodes of everyday life. In studying the actions that constitute episodes, one will be looking at how people produce the psychological phenomena, say, those agreed versions of the past we call "rememberings," which they can describe using the appropriate resources we have described in the local ". . . -ology."

People describe the things that they and other people do by the use of words like *anger, jealousy, decision, attitude,* and so on. Sometimes we use the words from the relevant ". . . -ology" in the creation of the phenomenon; for instance, to say "I remember . . ." is to perform a memorial act. But in other cases the words, such as *anger* or *jealousy,* are generally not used to display anger or jealousy. What do we find out by studying the words for emotions? Why not go directly to the study of the production of emotion in discourse? There is a relationship between the two studies, as we shall try to illustrate. The rules that we bring out in our study of the ". . . -ologies" of a culture are related to the ways in which we produce the phenomena. For example, the rules for the use of the word *anger,* in one of its many uses in English, must record the criteria for the correct use of the word, and therefore must reflect what someone is doing when they are acting angrily. Why then do we need to make video recordings of actual episodes of emotional upheaval and study their structure and try to identify their components? A display of anger does not arise spontaneously. It has a place in the sequence of acts that, in totality, constitute the episode. An emotionology will record the semantics of an emotional act, but we must also acquaint ourselves with the syntax of emotional episodes, so that we can understand the location of just this display at just this point in the events in question.

Language makes its appearance in discursive psychology in two ways. It is the medium of many discursive activities, particularly those we classify as cognitive. But it also serves as a basic model or analogue for analysis of episodes in which the actions are performed nonlinguistically, say, by postures and gestures, facial expressions, and so on, that is, by the use of other systems of signs. It is a main thesis of discursive psychology that episodes in which psychological phenomena are brought into being by the use of nonlinguistic signs should be analyzed as if they were through and through linguistic.

A Discursive Account of the Sense of Self

The Dual Context of Human Sciences

Human beings live in two worlds. One world is essentially discursive in character; that is, it is a world of signs and symbols subject to normative constraints. It comes into being through intentional action. That is the world that we claim is the proper subject of psychology as a science. The relationship of a person to that world is to be understood through the idea of skilfull action. A human being can live in the world of symbols and intentional normative activity only through the skills they have acquired, and thereby become and continue to be a person. There are two main kinds of skills that are often brought into play together and in complementary ways. There are manual skills, those we use to manipulate material stuff, and there are discursive skills, those we use in our symbolic interactions. Both manual and discursive skills are intentional and normative; that is, they are used for accomplishing some project or other, be it ever so small scale.

In this chapter we will not develop the idea of skills much further though we will return to say more about it later in the book. At this point we introduce it just so that we may have the basic idea of how individuals are related to their material and symbolic environments. The world of symbols is organized by the norms and conventions of correct symbol use. The other world in which we live, the physical or material world, is structured by causal processes. Our language is our main means for managing in the world of symbols, and our hands and brains are in the material world. It is characteristic of human beings to live in these two worlds. Philosophers have discussed the nature of this duality and treated it in many different ways during the last 400 years. We can find no convincing reason to accept the materialist view that the mental world is a redundant conception the study of which could be replaced for psychological science by investigations of neurophysiology. Nor do we accept the Cartesian way of explaining the dual nature of human existence in terms of the difference between a mental and a material substance, the one constituting the mind and the other the body. Discursive psychology is based upon a rejection of any form of Cartesianism. The mind is not a substance. The mentality of people comprises certain of their skills and abilities.

Of course, there could not be a world of symbols unless there was a material world. But these two realms do not reduce to one another. We cannot explain the world of symbols and how it works by reference to physical processes. Philosophers have called this relationship "supervenience." That is, there could not be languages and discursive processes unless there were brains buzzing with electrical and chemical processes and there were vibrations in the air and marks on paper. But those vibrations and those marks and those buzzings do not constitute the mind. They cannot explain the intentional character of symbol use and the normative constraints under which symbols must be used. A buzzing in the brain cannot be correct or incorrect. It can only be.

The Concepts of Personal Identity

If there is no mental substance, what could the self possibly be? When we turn to the psychology of the self, we are confronted with a bewildering variety of issues and problems. Let us begin with a few reflections on the remarkable fact that there are many languages into which the concept as we use it in English, expressed in the rules for the use of our word *self,* cannot be translated. It is very difficult to express the English idea of the self in Spanish. *Mi mismo* is used to make a reflexive reference to my personhood and does not imply the existence of anything other than myself as a person. It would not occur to a speaker of Spanish to substitute for *mi mismo* the word *alma,* soul. The French *moi-même* does not exactly mean "self" either. It does not have the Cartesian implication of reference to an inner entity, the substantial bearer of personal identity (Muhlhausler and Harré, 1991). The traditional French expression for that is *ego,* a noun created from a pronoun borrowed from Latin, the transformation of the grammar from that of an indexical to that of a substantive passing unnoticed. So it is not obvious that equivalents for this word can be found that are used in closely similar ways in other languages. Nevertheless, we do believe a sense of personal identity is a common feature of the psychologies of all human cultures at all times. But we do not believe that the hypothesis of a Cartesian mind-substance is the best way of accounting for the phenomenon.

Clearly, the sense of self, and the role of concepts of selfhood, are closely tied to personal identity. Identity, in the context of human individuals, has two aspects. There is what we are going to call the fact of personal identity: that is, that each human being other than oneself is taken by oneself, ceteris paribus, as an individual person, readily identifiable as such. When we examine that notion, we find that that too has two facets. I might be interested in what makes you a unique individual, one and only one person.

Philosophers have discussed this question a great deal. What are
the criteria by which I decide that you are one and the same individual as the individual I met previously? How do I pick you out
from a group? The identity of the body seems to be the dominant
criterion in practice, supplemented in hard cases by continuity of
memory. But I might be interested in what sort of person you are.
People fall into types. These types appear in our discussions of
other people and reappear in our beliefs about ourselves. Interesting though a study of the foundations of person-directed discourse
in the second and third persons may be, there is another aspect of
selfhood that has mostly been ignored by psychologists. That is the
nature and origin of the sense of personal identity that one has of
oneself. What is it for me to be an individual to and for myself?
Again, there are two facets to this phenomenon. There is the question of my individuality to myself, my sense of uniqueness. In what
does that consist? Then there is the question of what type of person
do I believe myself to be? Unfortunately, the word *identity* has
been used in psychology almost always for formulating the second
problem. An identity crisis, as it is understood in psychiatry, is a
situation where someone is uncertain about what type of person
they are or that they want to be. It is not a case of worrying about
which person one is. One's cluster of beliefs about oneself has been
called the "self-concept." In studying this fluid and fluctuating
self-concept, psychologists have not paid attention to the sense of
individuality without which the discursive presentation of beliefs
about *oneself* would have no anchor and would have nothing to
be about. Only by adopting the discursive viewpoint will it be
possible to develop a psychology of the self directed to the question of our sense of personal individuality and to undertake a study
of how we acquire it.

The distinction between the two ranges of questions about human individuality can be brought out in the following way: Consider how I might find out which person you are. I would try to
find out your name, where you come from, your job, and so on.
But notice that I can be wrong about any of these matters. Running across a couple of bearded foreign gentlemen in the British

Museum Reading Room, I could have thought that Marx was Engels and Engels was Marx. Which person you are, for me, is an empirical question. But what about the question of which person I am for me? Could I be mistaken about who I am? Could I wake up one morning and say to myself (whosoever that might be!), "I've discovered I have been wrong about myself all these years, I am not the person I thought I was. I am after all you." This is not just strange—it is incoherent. To make the remark, there must be a sense in which I am still myself. What has slipped here? My sense of my own individuality is not something I once discovered by observation, which I can check up on by taking a peek from time to time into my inner being. I do not think that one day when I was lying in my cradle I discovered that I existed. Hume argued long ago that we cannot explain the sense of personal individuality we have of ourselves, by looking into ourselves for some entity that is our self and of which all our thoughts, feelings, and so on are attributes. A little later, Butler pointed out that the idea that my sense of self comes from a coordinated string of memories will not do as an account of the sense of self either. For the thought of anything I have done to count as a memory presupposes that I know that it is a recollection of one of my experiences, actions, and so on. The self is somehow presupposed in the sense of personal identity. It is not discovered.

The "Self" in Discourse

Having identified the problem, which psychologists have generally been disinclined to investigate, and indeed have been prevented from investigating by the dominance of the experimentalist approach to method, let us see if we can make any progress by turning to a study of the means a person employs for the discursive presentation of oneself as a self, a unique person. We must begin with a hypothesis about this "sense of self." To have a sense of one's personal individuality is to have a sense of having a place or places in various manifolds, that is, systems of locations. To have a sense of myself as a unique individual, I have a sense of a location in space, literally a point of view. Strawson (1959) built his theory of individuality and personhood upon this feature of the sense of personal identity. But I also have a sense of existing at a moment in an unfolding of time, of my life as a trajectory or path through time. But there is yet another aspect to my sense of identity, at least in cultures influenced by the Judeo-Christian moral system. I have a sense of my responsibility as an agent. I am located in a network of mutual obligations and commitments to a manifold of other people and even to some animals. Finally, I have a social place, a location in a manifold of persons, ordered by status, age, reputation, and the like. To have a sense of self is to have a sense of being quadruply located, of having a place in four coordinated manifolds. I experience myself not as an entity but as having a place from which I perceive, act, and am acted upon and where I am myself perceived. That is a sketch of the phenomenology of selfhood, how I feel myself to be. It is no wonder psychologists did not try to study this phenomenon. It is clearly not susceptible to experimental investigation, and it is presupposed in all other studies of persons and personalities.

If, however, we adopt the principles of discursive psychology, and base our investigations of the hypothesis that the mind of any human being is constituted by the discourses that they are involved in, private and public, we need not despair of making an empirical study of personhood, of the nature of individual selfhood, just because the sense of identity is "subjective." We can turn to study how a person's sense of being uniquely located is discursively displayed. We can study how selfhood is produced discursively.

What aspect of a conversation would that require us to investigate? The use of pronouns would be an obvious starting point. In studying the use of first and second person pronouns, we are investigating the discursive production of selfhood. We shall illustrate this kind of research by briefly sketching the basic features of pronoun grammar by making an analysis of the use of pronouns in English as an example.

There is no special reason for starting with English. It is convenient for us because we are both native speakers. But we must beware that when we look out at other languages from this vantage point and see them as varying from English we must not take English as any kind of standard from which the other languages deviate. If we were Japanese discursive psychologists, we would start from Japanese grammar of the indexing of person in Japanese discourse and see other languages as varying from that standpoint. There is a problem with choosing English as a starting point that one runs into in studying pronominal systems. It has the second most restricted system of pronouns of all the languages that are easily accessible for study. Only *Inuit*, the language of the Eskimos, is poorer in indexical expressions. Inuit has only two pronominal devices, one that indexes a speech-act with the location and commitment of the speaker and one that indexes a speech-act with the locations of persons other than speaker. English has undergone a steady erosion of its pronoun system, and consequently an impoverishment of resources for the presentation of self. The most elaborate indexical system seems to be that found in Japanese. The precision and power of the person-marking force of the pronominal system in that language is such that Japanese people generally omit pronouns from everyday speech. The resources of Japanese are such that in a conversation between two Japanese people using pronouns and verb inflections something like 260 different social relations between them could be represented. Not all of these possibilities are actually used. Other languages make available person-marking refinements on other dimensions. For example, there are languages in which not only the second but also the first person is inflected for gender. Using this resource the content and social force of speech-acts could be marked for the sex of the speaker and addressee. In Japanese there are some pronouns generally used only by men, and some used only by women. For instance, *boku* is the first person form that is used by men to express solidarity while privately believing in superiority. We are informed that *boku* has migrated from student talk to the talk of men in general. Feminists have come to use *boku* to express a certain social and political attitude, that of equality with men. One can see how this use by women is derived from the student use.

Despite the fact that we are starting with a language that we know very well to be primitive in its pronominal resources, we will find the main outlines of the discursive psychology of selfhood illustrated in its indexical system. A brief sketch of the grammar will be enough to illustrate the point we want to make. An *anaphoric* pronoun is one that stands for some word, often a proper name or a definite description. In English *he* and *she* are typical anaphoric pronouns because they refer back to some person referring expression with which the discourse in question begins. For example, "*The pilot* came out of the cockpit and walked around the cabin and *he* said, 'How is everything back here?' and then *he* went back." All these "he's" have their referential force from links that are internal to the discourse. Only the expression "the pilot" denotes an entity outside the discourse. "I" and "you" are indexical pronouns. We have already used the term *indexical* informally. There are several different meanings attached to this expression but for us it means that the pronoun or other indexical expression indexes the content or social force of an utterance with the spatial, temporal, moral, and social location of the speaker. Indexicals are sometimes called "shifters," meaning that the denotation of a word like *I* shifts from speaker to speaker. *He* does not because its meaning is fixed by the chain of anaphors that lead back to the original referring expression and so to the original referent. But the references of indexicals shift with the speaker. To illustrate one of the differences between anaphors and indexicals, if I say, "Rom Harré will pay for your lunch," unless you know that that is the name of the speaker, he is not committed to foot the bill. It would be a strange situation in which that form was actually used by a speaker of that name unless as a joke. Compare that with the effect of the same person saying, "I will pay for your lunch." In the indexical formulation, the use of the person pronoun *I,* the speaker does commit himself to paying. With an anaphor, the responsibility, in general, does not shift to the speaker, though there are one or two complicated exceptions. But, in general, with indexicals, responsibility is automatically assigned to the speaker.

If the word *I* is an indexical pronoun, what does it index? The notion of indexicality has a double-sidedness. First of all, to understand indexicals, such as *here, now, this, that, me, I, you,* to explain what they mean on a particular occasion, we have to know about that occasion and, preferably, we have to have been there. If one was present on the occasion of an utterance, one knows who has taken responsibility by their use of "I." But for our purposes as discursive psychologists, another aspect of the grammar of indexical expressions is important. Consider a simple utterance in the first person. Someone says, "I can feel a draft." There are two aspects of the statement to which the "location" of the speaker might be relevant. There is what it tells us about the world, that is, the empirical content of the utterance. The draft is to be felt at the place at which the speaker is presently located. But how someone who hears this statement takes it also depends on how reliable they believe the speaker to be, in short, on the speaker's "position" or standing in the local moral order. Whether we believe the speaker to be reliable or unreliable, careless or meticulous, and so on will influence how we take what he or she has said. This aspect of an utterance is called its "illocutionary force." Considered with respect to this aspect, we can call an utterance a "speech-act." It is as if our utterances were prefixed with statements like the following: "Trust me—there's a draft," "I assure you that there's a draft," and so on.

It is the pronoun *I* that does the work of indexing these aspects of a statement with spatial locations and moral positions. My sense of self, of my individuality, is in part my sense of experiencing the world from a unique location in space, the location of my body. It is also, in part, my sense of acting on the world at that place, but also in relation to other people. My moral position is also implicated in my sense of my own agency. It is an essential component in the sense of self, and it is manifested in the role of the pronoun as that presents the speaker as a self. Personal identity is one's sense of being located in space and having a position in the moral order of the little group with which one is conversing. Our theory, then, is that selfhood is discursively produced for others by the use of the first person pronoun, and at the same time is discursively produced for ourselves. It reflects and in part engenders my sense of my own personal identity.

There is a complication that comes from our having used English as our model language. One's sense of self also involves one's autobiography, a fact that John Locke realized centuries ago. Of course, one's self could not be constituted by one's sense of one's own history, given that for an item to be classified by me as among the events of my life I must have a sense of my own identity to do it. Nevertheless, it is part of my sense of self to exist at just one moment in time and to have had a past and to hope for a future. But these temporal matters are not indexed by our English pronouns. We must rely on other indicators of time, such as the tenses of verbs and other indexicals like *now* and *then*. There are languages in which all this indexing work is done by the pronouns, for instance, the classical language of Java, Kawi, had such a system.

We want to elaborate this just a little, particularly with respect to the location in space. If one looks out from one's eyes and listens with one's ears and pays attention to the bodily tactile sensations of which one can become aware at this moment, one finds oneself at the center of a certain system of material bodies. One can also get a sense of oneself at the center of one's own material body. That, in a first approximation, is a beginning to an investigation of the structure of consciousness. One can become conscious of the fact that all that one perceives is structured around a kind of center, as Husserl (1973) called it, the "I" pole. But we cannot investigate the structure of consciousness publicly because each of these centered frames of awareness is private. But each individual's structure of consciousness, according to the tenets of discursive psychology, will appear in the way we converse. How? In the way *I* indexes what is said with the various positions and locations of the speaker. In the case we discussed above, the person was talking about something outside their body, a draft. But we can do just the same with things inside the body. My foot is farther from the physical center of my being than is my stomach, as we very well know. We both have the sense that for each of us the physical center of our consciousness is about two inches behind our eyes.

More Than One Self per Body:
The Power of Pronouns to Create Selves

To see the power of pronoun systems in the presentation of self, and how they can even override the uniqueness of a person's embodiment in just one body, we can examine a case of so-called multiple personalities, that is, a case where we become convinced that there is more than one self embodied in a particular human body. We can illustrate this point from the very first study of dissociation of personality by Morton Prince (1978 [1905]). It is a story of the many talks that took place between Dr. Prince and his patient, Miss Beauchamp. The interesting thing from our point of view is how Dr. Prince came to decide that Miss Beauchamp had a dissociated personality, or multiple personalities, and what were these "personalities"? Or to put the question in terms of discursive psychology, how did he decide that, in Miss Beauchamp's one body, there were three speaking persons? Looking at his reports of conversations from our point of view, it becomes very clear. There are three main pronoun systems in use by Miss Beauchamp. These can be set out in a table as follows:

Miss Beauchamp	Chris/Sally	Miss X
I	You	—
You	I	She
She	You	I

The third "self," Miss X, was never referred to by name by "Sally" nor did she refer to herself by name.

Morton Prince took the apparently disorderly speech of Miss Beauchamp and showed how it could be organized by reference to three independent pronoun systems, each presenting a different self. So when she spoke as "I," she would speak of things that had been done by "you" or "she." These were reported by one of the other selves, respectively, as things that "I" (Sally) or "I" (Miss X) had done or planned to do.

By using something like the above scheme, Morton Prince was able to make Miss Beauchamp's discourse completely intelligible. According to the point of view of discursive psychology, we would say that shows that this one body hosts three selves, self-1, self-2, and self-3. How do we know? Because the pronouns are indexically distinct. Each "I" indexes the same spatial location each time but they certainly do not index the same continuous sequence of times nor do they index the speech-acts of Miss Beauchamp with the same morally responsible agent.

We could imagine cases in which more than one body is required to sustain just one person. When we listen very closely to the symbiotic dialogue between mothers and small babies, in which the mother plays both parts, it begins to look rather like that. Morton Prince tried to get Miss Beauchamp to change her pronoun grammar. He demanded that when she wanted to refer to "you" (meaning Sally) she must use "I," and so on. He tried to fuse these diverse selves into one single discursive structure, around one single system of pronouns. By the end of the book he reports a certain degree of success. But we never know what happened to Miss Beauchamp.

We must be careful how we construe this example. It will illustrate very well the difference between the old idea of the self as something inside a person and the new idea of the self as a continuous production. It is not that inside Miss Beauchamp were three selves trying to get out. That is the old picture. According to the new picture, three selves or indexical centers were discursively produced. This is the psychological phenomenon. There are not three little egos inside Miss Beauchamp, each speaking up through her mouth. The speaking parts are all there is to it. They are the phenomenon, and these speaking parts are the selves.

Conclusion

The sense of self is an experience. The "discursive" thesis is that to experience oneself as having a location in a manifold of places and in relation to others is a necessary condition for being able to use and to understand indexical expressions. On the other hand, how does it come about that these senses of unique location are the salient features of selfhood? We do not believe that learning a language is what is responsible for our having the sense of physical location. It is the learning of perceptual and motor skills that is responsible for that. But it is expressed in the indexical grammar of "I." On the other hand, we do think that the sense of agentic position, the sense that one is the agent of one's actions and responsible to others for them, is something that we acquire through learning the language and the cultural conventions for the assignment of responsibility. So these aspects of the sense of self—physical location, temporal continuity, and agency—have different origins but they come together in the grammar. According to Vygotsky, the learning of manual skills is just as much a necessary condition for acquiring a sense of self as the learning of verbal skills. We believe that perception is a kind of manual skill. The ability to use your eyes is a bit like the ability to use your hands. In living our lives as members of a community that inhabits physical space and time, and assesses each of its members for reliability, these centerings come together. But in the interactions that stabilize and maintain our senses of identity, they are expressed in the ways we use our language, in particular in our use of indexicals.

❖ 8 ❖

Agency and Personality

They insisted we were less than we are for fear we might think we were more than we are.

Anonymous

In an effort to take on the mantle of a "science," psychologists dropped the use of the terms *action* and *conduct* and replaced them with the one term *behavior*, which was given a special physicalistic twist. This was all part of an attempt to "physicalize" the human mind. The latter term can be applied to atoms, lower animals, and meteorological systems whereas the first two seem to carry a sense of purposiveness. One acts for a reason, in order to do this or that, or as an expression of some attitude. Our interest is in intentional action, that is, action done for a purpose, though that purpose may be so routine that it is not consciously deliberated. If we can regard human beings as exhibiting at least some behavior that is of this type, that is, action or conduct, then it makes sense to draw on traditional concepts such as agency, responsibility, and character, all of which map our behavior onto some moral order.

The link between action and character shows why we might have chosen to amalgamate a discursive analysis of action with that of personality. Westcott expresses the relationship as he discerns it in the accounts of their own freedom given by various of his research participants.

In spite of difficulties in implementing their intentions, the actions they take are very much part of their conceptions of their own natures—my path, destiny, what is natural to me, what I really want to do. This is self-realization, but the practice of freedom is fraught with uncertainty, both the uncertainty of the propriety of the choices and the uncertainty of the success of the path chosen. But they assume responsibility both for the choice and the consequences of the choice. (Westcott, 1992, p. 27)

He has adopted a method in which he asks individuals about their experiences of individual freedom and tries to make sense of these against their historical, social, and cultural backgrounds. He concludes that freedom is a discursive activity. It is something that one does, that is, makes manifest in what one says about one's life.

Human freedom is not something that one has; human freedom is something that one does. One negotiates, constructs, and practices human freedom differently at different times and under different circumstances, with varying degrees of success. (Westcott, *loc. cit.*)

Our task is therefore to locate this idea of freedom in a psychological understanding of human individuals so as to make the questions of freedom, agency, and personality part of an inquiry that is personal and discursive. It begins by charting the ways in which we can begin to think of individual people as agents, active in the production of their contributions to a larger discourse.

The Discursive Agent and Social Causation

Human individuals are trained to use words and other signs, that is, to think conceptually. That training involves a mixture of coercion, persuasion, social structuration (Giddens, 1984), and so on and results in the individual being able to recognize and to conform to certain norms of signification operating within an area of discourse (Foucault, 1972). These norms not only determine what it is to understand something according to a given signification but they also validate certain ways of seeing situations. For instance, a Western scientist would perhaps take a certain experience to be that of being in a rain forest. This would imply that one was surrounded by a number of trees and plants none of which had any intentionality toward oneself (although one might credit various species with certain needs). The scientist might appreciate the plight of the rain forest and the threats to its survival and that of the creatures living within it but would be unlikely to experience (conceptually, at least) a sense of there being personal forces (such as Gods or Spirits) extant within the denizens of the forest or the forest itself. He would probably be ridiculed if he thought those things. To a tribal dweller in the forest, however, that scientifically ridiculed view would be self-evidently true and its confirmation would be found, for instance, in feelings engendered by the forest (which, to some extent, might be shared by the scientist but otherwise attributed and therefore essentially changed). The appropriateness of the personalized and animistic way of thinking of the forest might also be confirmed by things that happen as a result of certain kinds of action people take in the forest. This framework or discursive context offers different possibilities for thought, and therefore for conceptually structured action, to the scientist and the forest dweller. It also offers different frameworks of moral evaluation for the actions performed by each.

Let us continue for a moment the development of this scenario so that we can discern some of the strands that might go into a discursive understanding of the content and causes of actions. Our scenario is differently structured by two different discursive orders. In each there are certain checks and balances. In the one there is a sense of ecological responsibility and perhaps even the idea that the planet Earth is a superorganism, Gaia. To the scientifically trained ecologist, however, the fundamental reality of the rain forest is a system of objects that have various properties amenable to human exploitation. Against this background the forest dweller's view is fundamentally mistaken. The scientific "adviser" perhaps attempts to convey this by "educating" the tribe. Only too often the enthusiastic educator is horrified by the way the members of the tribe abandon all their reverence for the forest and treat it as a resource to be used for relatively short-term satisfactions. Here we see a person who, by making an apparently nonevaluative shift in the knowledge structure of a discursive group, produces a set of significations in that group that have, for him and one suspects ultimately for them, a profound moral impact. By conveying the Western "objective" specification of the eco-context of the tribe, he has made possible a set of actions and validations of actions that were checked in the preexisting discursive order.

We cannot say that the one set of evaluations and significations is unproblematically better on every possible dimension of appraisal than the other. After all, the Western conception has done much to alleviate certain kinds of human hardship. But what should be immediately obvious is that choices, actions, responsibilities, and the relation of an action to character can only be analyzed in the context of a total discourse. A man who cuts down a tree believing it to be the home of a forest dryad who will thereafter wander homeless through an inhospitable world acts differently than a man who cuts down a tree believing it to be only a source of wood to earn an income for him and his family. The latter may shift his moral ground nearer to the former if he subsequently comes to see himself as a profiteer from the rape of Gaia, but he will never occupy the same ground of signification as the first.

The training that inculcates ways of signifying constrains the reasons we can adopt for acting thus and so and disposes us to judge according to certain evaluative norms. But this process is as much facilitatory and empowering as conforming and restrictive.

For instance, take the use of the word *handle*. Once someone has understood this concept and introduced it into the articulation of their behavior, they can do things that otherwise they could not do. This person has clearly been shaped into adopting a practice and, in respect of that practice, is not free to choose how they will respond but can choose to discard the practice altogether. The choice to discard a way of thinking has real costs in terms of adaptation to a world where handles can be used to do all sorts of things. Thus someone's commitment to the discourse involves a relinquishment of freedom at a certain point but a consequent attainment of an ability that otherwise they would not have. Their use of the technique involved in the practice will, in fact, always show this tension. They will remain disposed to see things as handles under certain conditions and will thereby be enabled to relate to the environment in certain ways.

Before we go any further, we should specify the difference between this understanding of human behavior and the view that our activity is under stimulus control from things around us (including utterances). The theory of stimulus control is part of an approach that sees all things, including human beings, as objects that are caused to behave thus and so by forces acting on them. The picture is that there are internal forces that dispose us to act for certain goal-states and external conditions that differentially select which of our actions are likely to realize those states. The understandings and ways of thinking that we have mentioned are either ignored or treated as no more than conditioning structures that interact with stimulus inputs to determine which responses are exhibited.

It emerges from this theoretical construction of human behavior that there is a thoroughgoing causal chain (albeit complex) producing my behavior and that the self-conceiving subject (upon whom our evaluations are focused) is not part of the explanation of that behavior.

When this view of human behavior is imposed on the wider context of sociocultural explanation, the agency of the individual shrinks to that of an insignificant cipher responding to and constituted by the concurrence of structural forces and social conditions.

The task for discursive theories of agency is therefore to reinsert the agent into the story, the one who initiates the action, the one who, in some way, is significant in giving meaning to what he or she does and who they are. It is not sufficient to acknowledge a certain agnosticism about the inner causes of behavior and to rely on someone attesting to the things that have influenced their choices. We must find a way of understanding a person as an individual focus of discourse and as having a productive role in their own conscious activity.

Rule-Following and Intentionality

We have noted that, in shaping their behavior so that it realizes a rule, people tend to take normative attitudes to their own dispositions and responses. We have argued that these are copied from the responses that others make to an actor's responses, just as the responses themselves are copied (Harré, 1987a). In this view, there is a natural progression from "I have done this or that but mother/father/teacher/Freda thinks that is wrong" to "If Freda were here she would think that what was done was wrong in these conditions." The next step is to "Maybe doing this here is wrong," or "I had better not do that" or "I wouldn't think of doing that." This natural progression of the ability to comment on one's own actions highlights the normative attitudes to one's own responses that lie at the heart of the *"is right"/"seems right to me"* distinction central to rule-following (Gillett 1993; Pettit, 1990). It emphasizes that, above and beyond my own dispositions to react thus and so, I structure my activity in the light of *prescriptive norms* or *discursive validations*, which tell me how I ought to respond if I wish to be understood in this or that way.

In conceding that such norms structure my relation to the world so as to realize in me the terms of those discourses in which I am engaged, we do not imply that I, the active subject who declares myself for or against various positions and commitments, can be excluded from the explanation. If we were after a causal explanation of my responses then it would be important to adopt such a stance but in discursive explanation I am not eliminated from the process of structuration. It is my evaluations of my own activity that are the ultimate effective source of semantic conformity. As semantics (or meanings) are the core of intentionality and we are discussing intentional action, I am therefore a participant in and not merely an object of social causation. And it is my commitment to the course of action, and the implicit evaluations that define a given action as the action that it is, that produces that action. If I withdraw my commitment then it is not my action. We can illustrate this thesis by a brief discussion of weakness of the will.

Weakness of the Will

Weakness of the will is a considerable embarrassment for certain theories of mind. If, for instance, one regards the mind as a rational preference-serving mechanism that causally produces behavior, then it is difficult to understand the fact that human beings sometimes act as they would prefer not to. If one regards the mind as merely a drive-satisfying comparator that allows the winning drive to select an appropriate form of behavior for its satisfaction then it is also hard to understand how one can do that which is, all things considered, not what one wants to do. Any system that regards our "reasons" (including motives, desires, and moral attitudes) as causal states involved in a straight competition for the control of overt behavior has problems with the common phenomenon of doing what we wish not to do. Plato (1982) and Aristotle (1925) referred to this as the problem of *akrasia* or incontinence of action.

Plato considered that real weakness of the will was impossible. He thought that the akratic or incontinent agent was ignorant of the real worth of alternative courses of action and mistakenly opted for the one he should not have. But this manifestly does not do justice to the common experience that people can act on some intention that, even at the moment of action, they would regard as inferior to its alternative. Aristotle came closest to solving the problem by realizing that the skill of doing what one knows to be best is just that—a skill. He remarked that reasons to act thus and so had to be adopted as the determinants of behavior in order to be effective and that, if one did not have this skill, evident in those who demonstrate practical wisdom, then it was useless trying to reason one out of one's irrational or suboptimal behavior. He remarks, "If water makes a man choke, what can you give him to wash it down with" (Aristotle, 1925, Bk. VII.3) or "the incontinent man is like a city which passes all the right decrees and has good laws, but makes no use of them" (Bk. VII.10). The implication is that giving the incontinent agent more reasons to do the right thing is not going to help him. Rationally structured content used in recommending or validating the preferred course of action is not what the incontinent agent needs. The problem cannot be solved merely by adding rational or causal weight on the right side of the scales. That is why it confounds accounts of action that depend on the summation of causal influences with those that emphasize the determination of action by rational syllogisms.

We would say that overcoming akrasia involves a discursively learned skill of regulating one's behavior so that it conforms to the rule-governed significations one endorses in a given context. The agent may have formulated a syllogism that favors a certain (here rational but vicious) action, such as in the following:

1. I would rather succeed than be swayed by altruism or mercy.
2. The successful path requires me to ignore this person's need.
3. I will ignore this need and act for my own advantage.

It is a further question, however, whether this syllogism will actually guide the agent's intentional action. It is possible that a person might not have the skill of self-management required to carry the syllogism through. The relevant skill, like all others, is vulnerable to those things that throw us off our stride. They include immaturity or inexpertise, disruption by interfering factors such as emo-

tionally charged experiences, and reevaluations or sudden refor-
mulations of intention that, even if they do not alter the evaluations in play, may make an individual revert to an unfavored
intention. But the more skilled the agent becomes, the more these
challenges can be safely negotiated. In any event, the implications
for our account are clear: Acting in accordance with one's moral
and personal commitments is a learned ability in which one mas-
ters the structuring of one's activity according to one's own discursive positionings.

Rule-Following and Agency

We have argued that the essence of psychological activity is rule-
following. Where this involves socially or culturally mediated content (as most human thought does), the rules embed shared norms.
But rule-following is an inherently paradoxical activity. In being
trained to follow a rule, a person is equipped with a disposition to
respond to certain conditions in certain ways but is not causally
compelled to do so (Wittgenstein, 1953, sec. 195). The linguistic
or semantic response to a given situation does not simply depend
on a causally induced effect of physical features on the agent but
depends rather on the structure that is needed to form and enun-
ciate the agent's reasons for acting in a certain way. Thus Davidson
argues that there is *autonomy of meaning* whereby "once a sentence is understood, an utterance of it may be used to serve almost
any extralinguistic purpose" (Davidson, 1984, p. 164). This implies that rule-governed meanings (significations) are combined in
ways that do not simply cause a behavioral response in a given set
of conditions.

We could say that the rule gives a thinker the tools to formulate
certain reasons for action. It does so by giving them an adaptive
and discursive reason to organize their activity in certain ways.
The reason is the advantage attached to the use of a technique that
has an established signifying role in the structure of social adaptation by their linguistic group. The evaluations and relationships

within that discursive context give an actor a reason to incorporate a given range of semantic or meaningful responses in their manifest behavior in certain conditions but neither the rule, nor the context, nor any set of conditions compels a person to behave thus and so in a mechanical or crudely deterministic way. One makes a rule-governed response in certain conditions because that response will usually empower one to exploit some feature of a situation. One may choose to use or not use that power for any of a number of reasons (and any of those reasons might or might not be the kind of thing that would be endorsed by most of those sharing the social context/discourse). Someone might, for instance, just be non-conformist, contrary, or perverse. Their behaving thus and so by exhibiting certain meaningful activity is therefore (as Davidson notes) not subject to lawlike or scientific generalizations that exclude the need for reference to their own commitments and states of mind (1980, p. 217). Such features of a person's subjectivity, *ex hypothesi*, implicate them as a situated agent or subject and are therefore part and parcel of an understanding of events in which people think this and that and do this and that for reasons that they find worth acting on.

Types of Causation

Social *causation,* if we persist in using the term, is very different than ordinary (physical science/billiard-ball) causation. Discursive contexts inculcate the use of certain symbols that tend to structure the responses of individuals. Once the use of those symbols has been mastered, their connection to certain conditions is as *signification* but not as causally produced effect. The symbol or sign mediates semantic responses to presentations. In these responses people aim to be true to a practice located in a discourse in which they participate. An individual's semantic response is a *signification* and in making it the person takes an active role in structuring their domain of activity. Thus an individual actively structures the field of his or her own action according to the symbols available to them in a certain discourse (which represents a contemporary and socially informed restatement of what is, in effect, a Kantian thesis). Such a discourse makes certain responses available but also, by its practices of validation (which give hegemony over decisions to this or that person or consideration), constitutes some subset of those responses as dominant for the individual subjectivities within it and therefore it determines, in part at least, the way people relate to their world.

This view does not credit the human agent with any implausible freedoms. For instance, in general, an agent cannot simply choose the context within which they are born and subsequently live. There is therefore an important productive effect on a person's activity of signification by the conditions and discourses in which they develop their psychological constitution. Ultimately there will be customary and widely endorsed practices that do, in fact, constrain someone in that he or she is an agent with a certain historical, cultural, and mental position; these will both form the person and influence what he or she can become.

However, the individual, whose intentions are structured by and emerge from the positions taken up in a social context and the discourses that pervade and structure it, is able to choose the rule-governed techniques that they will use to organize their psychological responses. Thus their commitments or positionings within discourses that they adopt in making them become formative of their personality, which increasingly reflects certain discursive contexts and positions but no one is perhaps irrevocably bound by them. In this sense, there are effects or forces that may be discerned in the activity of an agent and are attributable to social structures. But these effects and forces are misconceived if they are represented as being similar to those at work in Newtonian mechanics. The relation of symbol to brain function and brain function to behavior is more subtle than a simple causal production. Conceptual structure, arising in discourse, both constrains and makes available ways of using information that equip an individual to take genuine initiatives in their life contexts.

Therefore social causation is a "strange beast," as it appears in the explanation of human behavior. It reflects the compulsion that discourse introduces into my relation to the world but is radically dependent on my consent to follow the "ought's" to be found at work in the (shared, interpersonal) rules governing meaning. And, of course, although one *ought* to judge and act thus and so, notoriously one does not always do so, even if almost nothing tells against it.

Social Causation and the Conception of Freedom

It is a small step from these reflections on human action to a conception of human freedom and individuality that does justice to our positioning within discourses (which necessarily involve relations of power).

In any discourse there are significations that are validated and others that are not. We have already discussed the nature of rule-following and the way in which it makes a variety of responses available to a person. We have hinted at the fact that the normative and evaluative structure of a discourse may constrain the ways in which a person acts. Consider the following case.

> George feels inadequate to cope with the stresses and challenges he meets daily. But he feels that he must be a successful man so as to be able to respect himself and command the respect of his others, particularly his wife. What is more, the cultural discourse to which he belongs tells him that his success is in his own hands, that a real man is in charge of his own life. However, he fails in a number of ways, in his schooling, in his job, in his own perception of how his wife and parents see him. Frustration, hostility, aggression, and ultimately violence result from this mismatch and he falls into a pattern that brings him into conflict with the law, breaks up his family, and blights the life of his children.

Now, what can we say about George? He has organized his world in terms of certain meanings. They include being a real man, being competent and able to cope with life, being successful. When it emerges that there are things he cannot cope with, that he is not as he portrays himself to be, these meanings provoke a certain kind of reaction. He sees himself as hurt or threatened and frustrated in what he would like to do and be. He reacts to this in ways that are validated within his discursive context. In certain contexts he would feel all-consuming shame and perhaps see no alternative but to destroy himself. Instead, he develops aggressive responses, which he then turns on others. The conceptual connections available within the discursive context he inhabits make his responses likely but do they make them inevitable? Is he free to react differently? The answer, as for almost all important questions, is "yes and no."

The traditional approach to the question of freedom has taken for granted a certain metaphysical background, or conception of the way things are in general, and attempted to argue within that. The dominant view of how phenomena come to be has been that of physical science. This view portrays human beings as some special kind of (inert) object that requires being moved by causal pushes and pulls that are based in the external world as mediated by the internal workings of human physiology. In the discursive view, this is no more than a conceptualization or signification of things and suffers the limitation of any discourse. The phenomena being observed are cast into a form that is validated in that discourse: here, cause and effect and the action of forces on bodies. This sets up the traditional problem of freedom. We feel ourselves to be free, to be somehow in control of what we do and responsible for this or that action, and yet we are told that all our movements are under the control of forces of this or that type. The discursive analysis of this problem does not accept that this is a necessary starting point.

We note first that the discourse of the natural sciences is formed by an intention to predict and control and therefore is bound to see every phenomenon on which it turns its investigative eye as exhibiting a character that is apt for (external, objective) prediction and control. Now, for the most part, this approach is sustained by successful observation of lawlike regularities in the phenomena being studied. Such lawlikeness grounds a way of thinking about natural phenomena in terms of forces and causal connections that can be discerned and exploited to achieve predictable outcomes. When we turn to human behavior, however, we find no such predictability. We do not even find generalizable laws that have any more than a minimal contribution to make to the analysis of a situation (Mischel, 1968). Instead, we find people apparently making their own commitments and forming their own conceptualizations, which seem to have an important role in determining what they do. Of course, this does not fit the model and so the phenomena are disregarded in favor of our general commitment to the view that the lawlike regularities must hold. It has been argued that we support this view by constructing, in the psychology laboratory, a minimalist world in which the responses open to people are so simplified that their actions have the appearance of the effects of causes. Jean-Paul Sartre and the existentialists were the first to argue that the formulation of general theories could not be allowed to obscure the phenomena as they revealed themselves in existence. If one takes careful note of the point at which one is located and refuses to allow theories of any sort, whether philosophical or scientific, to do away with what stands out as real in experience, then one is beginning at the right place. In the face of the general unpredictability (within any rigorously physical-type theory) of human behavior and the clear testimony of ordinary human beings about their ability to control their own behavior, it would be rash to continue to wear the sight blinders of object-oriented psychology.

In its place, we should become sensitive to the human experience of freedom and what impairs it (as Westcott, 1992, suggests). When we do this we find that there are all kinds of limitations, such as weakness of the will, that affect our abilities to do what we would choose were we truly in command of our own lives. But this does not amount to a general abandonment of the idea of self-control or freedom of action. Instead, it suggests that we look at people psychologically in terms of the ways in which they do, and can be enabled to, assume some control over their actions. The crucial factors that influence that ability or attainment of freedom in real-life situations then emerge as having a great deal to do with discourse, positionings, and validations operating within discursive contexts.

Validations give a person a reason to opt for one orientation to or way of thinking of a situation rather than another but they also determine what counts as a reason for acting in this or that way. Thus they not only make available but also recommend commitments to certain positionings within discourse. If these validations were reasons that one could factor into a decision in the way traditionally conceived, then we would be able to understand an individual course of action as the outcome of a balance of reasons. However, we have already seen that reasons alone do not determine how one behaves. In fact, when we considered the constraints on George's understanding and interpretation of his situation, it became clear that there were a number of actions that were just not open to him.

The positionings we take up in a discursive context lead to certain ways of construing what happens to someone and predispose them to certain reactions and attitudes to those significations. If I construe what is happening to me as threatening then certain responses are closed off. I cannot, for instance, take relaxed pleasure in the situation. If I am in a context in which people who have a different color skin are seen as inferior in culture, intellect, and moral character, then it becomes difficult for me to commit myself to such people in the ways I would to people of my own race or I might have to think of myself, as Huck Finn did, as a "dirty abolitionist." But, as we have noted, these significations are all revisable. As I enter into different discursive contexts, I come into contact with different ways of conceptualizing and reacting to the same conditions. I must then position myself in relation to these possibly conflicting ways of construing events. It is tempting to say that it is a person's character that determines the direction of adaptation but we must also realize that one's character is part of the commitment one makes.

Certain types of relationships and interactions will enable different responses to be made to discursive intersections and tensions. Some people will be unskilled in balancing competing meanings and submitting themselves to the reflective or challenging scrutiny that leads to revision of character and positionings, and others will be capable of doing that. We would favor the view that certain kinds of discourse facilitate and make available movement and negotiation in relation to the meanings that inform one's behavior. These tend to be found in contexts in which the intersection of discourse and the dialogue between patterns of signification is itself a validated type of activity. If individuals are affirmed and exposed in nonthreatening ways to the alternatives presented by different constructions, then one would expect them to develop and be comfortable with the skills of discourse. If, alternately, they are threatened for any departure from a relatively rigid set of significations, then one would expect them to be unable to profit from discursive diversity. The metaphors of "space or room to be oneself," "flexibility," "openness," "a secure footing," and so on express the discursive content of the experience of freedom (Westcott, 1992). Each implies that a person both sees diverse possibilities of investing their life events with meanings and has the skill and confidence to take up those possibilities in action.

To act with freedom, the discursive possibilities that are potentially available to an individual must be affirmed, owned, and used in some practice. To be free of constricting situations and the intrinsically limited meanings that create them, the significations giving rise to them have to be resisted by the subject/agent. Given that a person is always trying to make sense of their life and the situations around them, they cannot just abandon their established discursive positionings and put nothing in their place. Alternative meanings have to arise and be validated in some way. For some individuals this validation may be more or less independent of any values evident within shared interpersonal contexts but for others the existence of a shared context for the new evaluations is crucial. To the extent one can negotiate, more or less on the basis of one's own discursive skills, which actions would most suit one's intentions in different contexts, one acts freely. In this case the way in which actions are suited to situations reflects and can only be understood by the commitments of the subject to significations and positions in discourse.

In general, to resist or affirm one discourse is to locate oneself in another and to be able to cope with the subjective tensions resulting from their contact in the individual mind. George has to be able to cope with the possibility of abandoning the self-conceptualizations that structure his action and identity if he is to reformulate and reform his activity. This brings us to the fact that acting freely involves a risk because it requires not only a reconstruction of aspects of behavior but also, in part, a recasting of oneself. To many people this is not possible and to some people it is not desirable. Whether their choices are free depends on the extent to which they are made on the basis of a selective commitment to the positions adopted. This condition can be defeated by a lack of knowledge of the choices available or a lack of the ability to seriously consider and perhaps commit oneself to a position different than the one that one already occupies. Both limitations can only be overcome in discourse, the one depends on its content and the other on its evaluative structure. Insofar as one makes these explicit to oneself and takes up some intentional attitude to them, one is doing what is involved in freedom and the details of the physical-theoretic account of what might be going on in one as that happens seem to take nothing from the reality as experienced.

We began this chapter by pointing to the relation between the idea of freedom and the construction of personality as a discursive activity. It is now time to turn to the second element in this relation.

The Identifiable Subject/Agent

The study of personality aims to account for the unique psychological profile of any given person. For this reason, the first step in discussing personality is to develop a conception of a person. In the traditional view, the conception of a person with which one operates determines what properties and variations in properties of things of that type might go into making each of them unique. The traditional view has therefore adopted a model of a person as an integrated system of processes and dispositions the nature of which can be revealed by probing the psychic interior of a person as subject and identifying differences between different specimens of *Homo sapiens*. But it is immediately evident that this is a typology allowing only groupings of persons in that any manageable set of dimensions of assessment is going to lead to a finite range of combinations of mechanisms or dispositions and is therefore not going to provide us with a specification of human uniqueness.

However, in thrall to the substance-property model of the mind, psychologists have continued to assume that tests of personality can reveal underlying internal variables. Most of these psychometric approaches fall under the broad rubric of trait theory whose proponents include Gordon Allport (1937), Raymond Cattell (1966), and Hans Eysenck (1953). These theorists tend to analyze psychometric tests in such a way as to produce factors that are based on clusters of items to covary, at least as they are represented in numerical scores. Each cluster is supposed to be the realization of an underlying trait. Once the clusters have been identified, a name for the posited underlying trait is derived from an inspection of the test items defining it. The names of some traits have a commonsensical meaning, such as submissiveness-dominance and shrewdness-forthrightness, while others are neologisms invented for the occasion such as introversion/extraversion. In most of these theories there are usually a conveniently small number of traits, somewhere between 3 and 30.

These "mental entities" (we will call them that for convenience) combine with each other to influence behavior in various ways and create predispositions to exhibit responses of various types. For Eysenck, the variable properties that he uses in defining personality are ultimately to be understood in terms of the balance of excitation in various brain systems. The activity in these brain

systems can be manipulated by using a variety of techniques to
some extent based on classical conditioning paradigms (Eysenck,
1985). The resulting dynamic balance of behavioral patterns can
sometimes be rendered more functional for the individuals subjected to such manipulations in a psychotherapeutic situation.

Trait theories are just one example of the search for inner mechanisms that explain individual differences in human responses to
different situations. They share with the whole range of theories—
known generally as dynamic theories—the view that the human
being is an object, subject to inner and outer forces that the psychologist must discover and make predictions about.

Freud must stand as the father of all dynamic theories of personality. In a sense, he created the terminology of all dynamic
accounts of personality by positing that the inner workings of the
mind functioned somewhat as a device for the channeling of energy. It is not our aim to survey personality theories in any depth.
That has been done by a number of authors (e.g., Ryckman, 1989;
Pervin, 1970). But it is instructive to consider the types of assumptions common to dynamic theories of personality so that we can
compare and contrast them with discursive approaches.

According to Freud, there are primitive forces or instincts at
work in the human mind that create pressure or energy aimed at
obtaining certain types of gratification. (Already we can see that a
number of somewhat incompatible physical models are at play in
the background of the theory.) This energy drives the organism to
act in ways likely to produce those gratifications. But Freud also
believed, somewhat paradoxically, that in addition to the *life instincts* concerned with hunger, thirst, and sexual needs there was
a *death instinct* that was responsible for aggressive acts. The instincts are, however, thwarted to some extent by controlling influences mainly arising from social settings (Freud, 1985) and expressed through the reactions and admonitions, praise and blame,
of parents, other adults, or social authorities. The controlling influences do not, however, remain external. They become "inter-
nalized" and make possible intraindividual control of the instincts.
This leads to a tripartite structure of the mind in which we find a

seething cauldron of steamy primitive instincts striving for expression or release. This is the Id. A rigid authority structure represses the expression of these urges. This is the Superego. Finally, there is a (partly) conscious, organized, psychic field on which this conflict is played out. This is the Ego. The Id needs to find ways of discharging its energy and the Superego needs to ensure that these ways meet the constraints imposed by social mores. The Ego is divided into two major domains, the *conscious* and the *unconscious*.

The unconscious mind has two subdivisions in that some of its psychic content is "preconscious," that is, capable of becoming conscious. Contents of the other subdivision cannot be admitted to consciousness. They form the unconscious "proper" (Freud, 1940). Those psychic entities that cannot be expressed are kept in check by Ego defense processes such as repression, denial, displacement, sublimation, projection, and rationalization. Defense mechanisms or processes are themselves largely unconscious although they express themselves in conscious behavior. Thus a person who is fascinated by cruelty to others might act in a very kindly and gentle way and express only kind and gentle sentiments as a reaction to their own underlying sadism. Another example would be the person who denies that they are ever sexually attracted to children and constantly speaks in the most sentimental and moralistic terms about the purity of children because unconsciously they have pedophilic desires. The problem is that the mechanisms do not really work and the forbidden instincts create tension in the psyche and try to break through so as to be expressed and gratified. Freudian theory gives rise to a popular model of the human actor, according to which people are seen as having a Jekyll and Hyde nature with the vigorous, primitive, hedonistic, and aggressive side being submerged behind a civilized veneer.

Freud's theory wholeheartedly affirms his own convictions about the deterministic nature of human behavior. In his view, we are all played on by causal influences that combine to set up a complex mechanism within us. These influences direct our responses to life situations. Much of this mechanism is unconscious and inaccessible to the rational or reflective self and definitely not amenable to control and direction by one's intentions as a conscious agent. The theory is, in fact, able to provide explanations that contradict a person's self-understanding because the most interesting causes of our dramatic and unusual behavior are, *ex hypothesi*, unconscious (not merely preconscious). On the basis of the division in the psyche and the unique configurations of mechanisms and processes that hold sway there, each of us has a different personality, the nature of which cannot really be discerned by self-report.

It is understandable that existentialists such as Jean-Paul Sartre should find this thesis unattractive. Their stress on human freedom, responsibility, and self-determination are entirely inimical to the Freudian approach. Sartre is led to argue that all the supposedly unconscious disturbances of the psyche that are alleged to lead to psychiatric disorders are, in fact, examples of "bad faith" (Sartre, 1958). An individual who is in bad faith is conscious of his or her internal conflicts and yet cannot admit them to self or others. Sartre contributes one philosophical strand to the reaction to psychoanalytic doctrine that seeks to preserve the freedom and dignity of the human being (it is interesting that a theory as opposed to psychoanalysis as Skinnerian behaviorism should be thought to have the same consequences in regard to human freedom). We all realize, however, that Sartre is perhaps too extreme. There are aspects of the psychological life of each of us that do not appear to be fully understood and articulated such that we are conscious of them but choose not to affirm them. The problem for an adequate psychology, which does not seek to turn the subject into a complex object or mechanism, is to account for these facts of our common experience and yet avoid the dehumanizing (or objectifying) move. It is obvious that such a psychology has direct relevance for our understanding of both freedom and personality.

Before we turn to a discursive account of personality, we ought to notice that there is a problem, shared by all the internal mechanism theories of personality, which a discursive view does not have. The discursive view of individuality and personality does not need to find a distinct constellation of inner processes to explain the uniqueness of each human being because every human being is given as unique in ways directly relevant to psychological explanation. Each human individual stands at a unique intersection point of human discourses and relationships. If these things are the ground on which a mind is built and the milieu in which it operates, then a discursive account need look no further for the basis of the uniqueness of an individual mind.

Personality and Cognitive Structure: A Revolutionary Formulation

George A. Kelly (1955) formulated a theory of personality that was totally opposed to the idea that a human being is a slave of inner forces. In fact, his approach is the first real attempt to accept the diversity of meanings that human beings give to their experience. He believed that human beings came to know something about the world and their own place in it by formulating interpretations of the world-as-they-experience-it. He claimed that a human being "is in a position to make different kinds of representation of his environment and so is not bound by that environment but only by his interpretations of it" (Bannister and Mair, 1968, p. 6).

Kelly called his basic philosophical position "constructive alternativism." He claimed that the universe and its contents were not susceptible to being known in some definitively true sense that corresponds to reality but only to being construed in various ways. Some of these are successful but others do not stand the test of our adaptive needs. He felt that the basic need of a human being was not one of or even a set of biological drives. It was the need to move toward the finding of increased meaning in our lives and situations. This cognitive need does not function like one of the inner forces or instincts of dynamic theory. Rather, it is an expression of the active nature of human beings who are continually seeking to understand and trying out ways of giving meaning to things around them. Thus Kelly's theory has been summarized as the view that human beings are scientists, forming hypotheses and theories about their world and trying to make sense of it.

Kelly regards the human being as making sense of the world by building systems of personal constructs.

> In building systems of personal constructs we place interpretations on events. Through an abstraction process, we construct the meaning of events for ourselves. (Kelly, 1955, p. 50)

The constructs one uses allow one to anticipate events in ways that recapture the useful features of similarly construed events in the past. The abstraction process mentioned determines which similarities and differences will enter into the content of a construct and thereby offers a set of reproducible strategies that may or may not prove their worth in practice. Having made the assimilations required to construct events in a certain way, a person is provided with a strategy for adaptive action. Thus the person as scientist is in the business of finding and refining useful ways of predicting and psychologically adapting to the challenges of life situations.

It is interesting to note how well Kelly does in characterizing the nature of science so as not to presume the physicalist or positivist model of psychology. Science, for Kelly, does not produce a reflection of the world as it exists in some objective, impersonal, or neutral medium. Rather, it produces an interpretation that equips us to anticipate and adapt to things that happen. Kelly would side firmly with those who deny that science aims at the single true picture of the world as a purely theoretical endeavor; for him the tests of adequacy of scientific representations are all related to one type or other of effective intervention (Hacking, 1984). This is, of course, quite compatible with having some kind of superordinate cognitive map of things such that one can determine whether, in terms of that map, a given representation is more or less accurate. In fact, if human beings are in the business of making sense of the world and their lives in it, then some overview rather than a mere repertoire of strategies would be decidedly advantageous.

The special difficulty that arises in relation to a scientific study of human beings is that there is, for Kelly, a scientist on both sides of the relation (between investigator and the thing investigated). This means that, in the case of human beings, the strategies for adequate intervention have an added factor to take into account— the real constructive activity of the person (subject) who is being studied. People are not inert and moved by forces in relation to which they are passive. They are moved, as Kelly is at pains to point out, by their own ways of construing events and objects and therefore by their various anticipations of the future in regard to those things. For this reason, the human sciences must come to terms not only with a description of the events that affect a person but also with the interpretations of those events by that very person. This entails that, for many purposes, the investigator must enter into dialogue with the subject and, of course, that dialogue will not itself be psychologically neutral in relation to the subject's thought and action. Furthermore, they enter into dialogue as "investigator" and "subject," but this is only one of the many role pairs they, as individual people, might adopt. And the perception of other aspects of their relationship may, of course, have an influence on any behavior that occurs in an experimental situation.

The realization that there is a shifting dynamic discourse between the subject and any experimental context is fairly damaging for the view that psychology fits the model of science according to which we must study fixed, definable objects and the impersonal forces acting on them. The fixed-object-passive-causality-lawlike-relation picture underpins our attempts to chart the objective properties of things with a generality and reproducibility that transcend any investigative manipulation. But this strategy seems highly inappropriate to studying people and may not be appropriate even in our study of animals and even the things and substances of the material world.

Kelly's investigative procedure does not need to have such a fixed target. In the framework created by the adoption of the " 'Man' as scientist" metaphor of Kelly's theory, each individual person is in constant negotiation with the world (Pervin, 1970). Each person puts different interpretations on things accordingly as they find it useful to liken them to the contents of this or that other experience from their past and, on the basis of these conceptualizations, they plan their future interactions with these things, people, and situations. If one's activities and projects do not work out in a way that is adaptive, one shifts one's interpretation and finds new dimensions of likeness and prediction. In this view, the "properties of things" become dynamic, fluid, filled with anticipation, and almost limitless in their possible variety. But each person is constrained by the need to make sense of or order experience in ways that aid adaptation. This, we would suggest, is a useful way to look at the abstraction and signification of psychological "properties" that is the aim of discursive psychology.

It is evident that an important part of Kelly's theory is that the human individual is active, not inert, in the face of experience. When a person perceives something, they do not merely receive impressions that give rise to beliefs. In perceiving, one confers meaning on a situation as a result of patterns of stimulation of one's sensory receptors and in accordance with successful past constructions. When a person thinks, he or she does not merely undergo a set of internal processes that perform calculations on data but searches for meanings by trying different moves between constructions of the world. This activity enables someone to find ways of making the most sense of their current situation (real or hypothetical) in the light of everything else they have experienced (and interpreted in the light of their constructs). When a person acts, they do not execute certain operations as a result of the thrust of this or that inner force. Human actors adopt constructions and use them to organize their activity in the light of the meanings they find in things.

This last set of observations brings us to the move to find meaning that seems central to Kelly's cognitive formulation of personality. Is this a substitute for the motivations and drives found in more conventional theories? Kelly did not think so:

> We do not specify nor do we imply, that a person seeks "pleasure," that he [or she] has special "needs," that there are "rewards," or even that there are "satisfactions." In this sense, ours is not a commercial theory. To our way of thinking there is a continual movement toward the anticipation of events, rather than a series of barters for temporal satisfactions and this movement is the essence of human life itself. (Kelly, 1955, I, p. 68)

We might regard this disclaimer as too sweeping but it surely redresses the imbalance created by many other theories of human psychology. It emphasizes the central place of active thinking and assignment of meaning in understanding the unique psychological constitution of each human being and also respects that individual as a participant and negotiator in the interpersonal domain of meanings.

Kelly's fundamental postulate was that "a person's psychological processes are psychologically channelized by the ways in which he [or she] anticipates events" (1955, I, p. 46). The person as psychological subject is thought of as forward looking, aiming to anticipate situations and therefore control and take responsibility for actions in those situations. This is done by developing constructs that focus on the similarities and differences between things. The greater the ability to build an organized system of anticipations and order them according to what the actor values, the greater is that actor's ability to act with assurance. If a person elaborates for him- or herself a system of interrelated constructs that have a wide range of useful applications in different experiential situations then that person will be well adapted to the world. Each individual has a unique ordering of such constructs and they vary in their modifiability in the light of new experience and in the ways in which they are applied to objects, including that very active subject. This cognitive constellation defines the individual and allows us to understand and relate to that individual as a self-defining agent.

Problems arise when an individual's construct system does not allow adequate adaptation because it fails to anticipate events or to assimilate them to other experiences in ways that allow organized action. This leads to maladaptation and distortion in one's constructs. One might, for instance, "un-name" a construct (make it "preverbal") or submerge one pole of the implicit contrast involved in a particular construction of events (Ryckman, 1989, p. 333). This does lead to tensions of various kinds. For each person, there is a core of constructs that defines his or her cognitive essence as a self-conceived individual, and significant departures from this in order to accommodate experience lead to guilt—a person is aware of not being who he or she sees him- or herself as being. A person might, in another case, find that events escape adequate construction and that they cannot cope so that anticipations fail and the capacity for adaptive action is lost. In this case, one will experience anxiety. But, unlike Freud, Kelly did not invalidate the self-conception of the subject to discover the nature of these psychic problems. In fact, he says, "If you do not know what is wrong with a person, ask him [or her], he [or she] may tell you" (Kelly, 1955, p. 322).

There are therefore many ways in which Kelly's theory is congenial to a discursive understanding of the mind. It remains to explore a dimension that is implicit but often underconceptualized in Kelly's theoretical writing by turning to the location of subjects in discourses.

A Discursive Reformulation of Personality

Kelly's approach is implicitly interpersonal in that his major assessment technique, the Role Construct Repertory Test, focuses on the way that people construe those who are closest to them. In this test, the person as psychological subject lists a number of people and then is asked to think of some way in which two of these people would differ from a third. The dimensions of distinction are personal descriptors and the relevant contrasts such as intellectual/boring, loving/unloving, aggressive/gentle, musical/

nonmusical, educated/uneducated. Each subject must then rate all of the people on their list on each of the constructs they have defined. This is of great interest to discursive approaches for several reasons.

1. The participant's own ideas are the basis of their assessment.
2. The constructs are defined by reference to real people to whom the participant relates in everyday discourse.
3. The interpersonal world of the participant is used to explore their own applications of their constructs and to provide the investigator with a framework against which to try to understand the judgments and classifications that that individual person makes.

We should also notice that the constructs are named by the subject suggesting that there is a link between the speech-act world and the use of constructs. We have already noted the norms and values that shape the discourses defining the speech-act contexts of any person, whether or not they are playing the role of psychological subject, and therefore we can observe that the means of assessment central in Kelly's understanding of personality tend to locate the subject in discourse. A discursive reformulation of personality emphasizes these features and links them in explaining the uniqueness of each human being.

People make self-constructive use of their discursive skills in that "the contents of human opinions, emotions, and motives are appropriated from the contents of our descriptive and evaluative commentaries on the natural and social world" (Greenwood, 1992, p. 37). In this sense, we are not as original and creative as a misreading of Kelly might suggest. We make use of the semantic content of various signifiers that have a use in the discourses to which we belong. Thus, for instance, a young man might adopt the idea of sexuality as a guiding construct, seeing himself as sexually powerful and women as sexual objects to be chased and conquered. He does not really see women as persons with their own perspective and identities to define but as targets for a certain appetite that he conceives of himself as having. For a character like Don Juan, this might be a dominant construct, defining his life in terms immanent, for instance, in the infamous "catalogue." In some of the critical or deconstructive reconceptualizations of psychology (Henriques et al., 1984), the whole idea of drives or needs might, as in Kelly's account, be displaced by concentrating on the meanings or images in terms of which people construe their own personalities.

In the discursive type of account, self-location within discourse is the key to understanding constructs and through them personality. People adopt or commit themselves to certain positions in the discourse that they then and there inhabit. For instance, someone might locate himself as "a rebel without a cause" in a discourse where the social context is seen as constricting or colorless and individuals have to stand out of that context and distinguish themselves. In such a case the widely shared rules and validations of this social context will provide this James Dean look-alike with a reason not to act in certain ways. He depends on and appropriates those meanings available in the discourse but tends to act in ways opposite to his perception of the general values that animate the discourses with which everyday life is constructed around him.

This account offers a way of understanding *akrasia*, or weakness of will, as an agent's acceptance of certain significations at one level but an inability to act in accordance with those meanings he or she most values. For instance, someone might see themselves as a detached, unruffled, self-moved mover, who does what they please in life without reference to the vulnerabilities, needs, and hopes of others. According to these significations, such a person should act without showing reactions to the opinions of others at certain points in their relations to them. However, this more sensitive and insecure self might occasion reactions that let that person down. One might find oneself getting upset, betraying a sense of threat, need, or embarrassment where the characteristics that constitute one's idealized self would not give rise to such reactions.

One might also find oneself making choices that would not be made by the aloof, separated-from-the-common-herd persona to which one aspires. This indicates that the person has not, in the context of those discourses in which he or she has participated, developed the skills to master the techniques that give real-life content to the significations they apply to themselves. The fact that someone's knowledge of these significations lacks its normal application to what they do in relation to a variety of situations means that they act in accordance not with what they judge to be best but according to other intentions incommensurable with their overall life project.

One can imagine this tendency arising in a number of ways. For instance, the "experts" who would normally impart discursive techniques may just not use certain significations and thus the individual might come in contact with certain meanings that are not grounded in practical life, for example, those involved in a romantic novel. Alternatively, the "expert" individuals may themselves not act in accordance with the significations they use. In the latter case the individual would be unable to attach an adequate contextual meaning to the signification as he or she lacked models or training in its actual use (this is, of course, just a different lack of grounding in practical matters). Consider the example of a child who is taught by implicit evaluations to regard an uncle as "a hard man." From another perspective and in the eyes of many persons, this uncle is a weak man who tends to shift his stance with shifts in the opinion of others and is not really "hard" except in his expressed opinions. The failure to act "hard" toward others undermines the actual meaning of that signification and yet the implicit evaluations suggest that it should be acted on. This leaves the child, as it develops and tries to locate itself in relation to discursive meanings, with an impossible task in a world where those meanings are, in general and necessarily, closely tied to manifest activity.

We should point out, however, that we are not replacing "inner forces" with "social forces." The centrality of the idea of the self-location of the agent in discourse removes this temptation. As we have noted in our discussion of rule-following, a person, whether in everyday life or playing the role of psychological subject, follows rules in order to make use of certain meanings in organizing their behavior. The role of the person in adopting rule-governed significations entails that we cannot merely replace forces with discourses so as, yet again, to negate the active agent in favor of extrapersonal explanations (of a social rather than internal type). Social causation disposes the person to certain reactions and ways of acting but does not determine that they will act thus or so. This means that we will be able to make statistical predictions of behavior on the basis of social variables but we will not necessarily be able to make sense of the actions and reactions of an individual in a particular situation. The latter project will only be amenable to a detailed, empathic, and individualized understanding of the way someone has construed and come to organize their own location in a range of discourses.

We have already suggested that the notion of the unconscious is best understood in relation to what can be affirmed and validated within a discourse. There are meanings justifiably assignable to what a person is doing that are either poorly mastered or incommensurate with the values arising from that person's discursive self-location as a conscious agent. These meanings have a validated use but it is not available to that very person, for reasons we might come to understand by appreciating the rest of his or her self-construction. The person whose actions evince these significations will therefore neither be in control of nor fully responsible for the things they are doing because they cannot adequately locate their content. For instance, a young woman who questions the way that her partner is managing their money might not understand why he cannot discuss this with her and he may come to regard her as being hostile to him. She may not consider this questioning as touching his worth as a person whereas he does. We would probably only come to understand his reaction by looking at the discourses that have determined his self-conception.

Conclusion

The discursive study of personality aims to understand the individual's self-locations and relate them to the discursive contexts in which they are formed and expressed. From this perspective, we give both credence and importance to the personal commitments of the subject and the meanings and positions he or she takes up. The fact that those features that explain a person's behavior are determined by that very person entails that there is a link between personality and freedom.

People operate with the meanings available to them in discourse and fashion a psychological life by organizing their behavior in the light of these meanings and integrating them over time. The result of the integrative project is a personality or character that is, to the extent permitted by the discursive skills of the subject/agent, coherent and creative. The ideal is a psychological life with the character of an artistic project and not merely a stream of experiences and responses to stimulation. Of such a life we might say that it has meaning in the same sense as a work of art has meaning. The meaning is no more summarizable in words than is a symphony or painting but it is discernible by those who are themselves well versed in discourses, their structures, and their interrelations. It is within this context that human behavior is able to be understood in terms of both breadth and depth (Taylor, 1964). A lesser conception of human beings and of psychology leaves us bereft of the components of such an understanding and fails to display the richness of the human mind and personality, which draw on meaning and value as determined within discursive contexts.

Emotion Words and Emotional Acts

Redirecting the Psychology of the Emotions

R ecently a new, discursive approach has quite transformed the
psychology of the emotions. The change has been brought
about in part by the development of the new style of psychological
research described in this book, the study of mental processes as
properties of discourses. There has also been a growing literature
of outstandingly competent work in anthropological psychology,
directed to the understanding of diverse and exotic emotion systems (Lutz, 1988; Rosaldo, 1980). The radical character of new-
style psychological research can be shown by contrasting it with
the point of view that stands in the strongest opposition to discursive psychology. The old theory of emotions, and the research

practice that went with it, was based on the idea that emotions are states of individuals and that they are felt physiological reactions to environmental stimuli. There are some who believe that these alleged reactions are the result of a Darwinian process of natural selection. The study of emotions would then be a branch of ethology, and explanations of the genesis of emotions would be sought for in physiology. This theory is connected with the thesis that there is a small number of basic emotions out of which all others are constructed. This view is completely rejected by the advocates of the new psychology. We think it is simply wrong, wrong in the way that the phlogiston theory of combustion or creationist theories of the origin of species are wrong. In explaining the discursive view, we hope it will become clear that the old theory completely misses the psychological problems of the emotions, because it fundamentally misconstrues the nature of emotions and their role in human life.

Some 20 years ago it was realized that there was an ineliminable cognitive element in the psychology of the human emotions. Which emotion a person took themselves to be experiencing depended on what they thought was the situation in which that emotion was experienced. How do we take this factor into account and yet pay proper due to the role of bodily feelings in the experience of many emotions?

Parrott (1993, p. 67) delineates two strategies through which this might be accomplished.

> One [strategy], the hallmark of the *dual systems* approaches to emotion, is to conceive emotion as having some noncognitive origin that may or may not subsequently lead to cognitive activity. The other, the hallmark of *cognitive appraisal* approaches to emotion, is to consider emotion as necessarily involving an appraisal of the situation which may or may not be biased.

But there is a third strategy. We might ask what are the functions of emotion feelings and displays in the episodes of everyday life? The answer from the point of view of discursive psychology is to treat these feelings and displays as being psychologically equivalent to statements. Primitive biological reactions to situations provide the basis of a kind of "vocabulary" of sign forms, in much the way that our nervous system and musculature offer us the wherewithal for making articulated sounds. But the point of giving a speech, say, outlining a program of tax cuts, is not susceptible to a *biological explanation*. It is a situated contribution to a discourse and depends for its effectiveness not only on the use of shared language but on a certain common background of knowledge and belief.

The emotions should not be thought of as abstract entities such as "anger" or "chagrin" but as actual moments of emotional feelings and displays, moments in which we are "feeling annoyed" or in which we are "displaying our joy" in particular circumstances in a definite cultural setting. Our focus will be on the role of these feelings and displays in the real-life episodes of daily existence.

Our first clue to the nature of emotions construed in the new way comes from noticing that not all body feelings or displays are emotions or are associated with the emotions. For example, if I groan and stretch and say, "I'm going to bed," I would be taken to be displaying tiredness, feeling tired, and so on, but nobody calls that an emotion. In no culture that we know of is "needing to go to the 'loo' " catalogued as an emotion! These are two striking and commonplace examples of bodily states and characteristic displays that are never taken as emotions. We need to be able to understand why that is so. The discursive theory has a ready answer. Feelings and displays are connected with emotions, or are to be taken as emotional, when they accomplish two things: they are embodied expressions of judgments, and, in many cases, though not in all, they are also ways of accomplishing certain social acts. For example, when one feels or displays envy, this is an expression of the judgment that someone has something that one would oneself like to have. In the case of malign envy, one judges oneself to have been demeaned or depreciated by the possession of that good by the other. To take another example, because a display of anger, irritation, or annoyance expresses a judgment of the moral quality of some other person's action, such a display is also an act of protest, directed toward the offending person.

An emotional feeling, and the correlated display, is to be understood as a discursive phenomena, an expression of a judgment and the performance of a social act. How does this effect psychological research? In addition to and of more importance than the charting of the bodily changes that occur before, during, and after an emotional display, we must ask what judgments they are used to express and what social acts they are used to perform. The same analysis is to be applied to emotional feelings, which are to be treated as private or *sotto voce* judgments.

Emotion feelings and displays as expressions of judgments lack premises. We are said to be overcome by grief, helpless with laughter, and so on. Unlike the conclusions of syllogisms, they rest on biological responses and cultural training, not on other judgments. Yet they can be rational or irrational, proper or improper, and so on.

This analysis has a striking consequence. If this account is universal, to be used in the study of all human forms of life, whether revealed by anthropologists or by historians, the undoubted fact of the diversity of the moral orders of humankind would lead us to expect that there would be just such a corresponding diversity in the local repertoires of emotions. The once popular emotion "accidie" is unknown to modern people. Indo-Europeans seem to have no place for the emotion the Japanese call "amae," with a display of which an adult Japanese expresses a kind of child-like emotional dependency that we would treat as a mark of immaturity.

Cultural studies reveal another dimension of variation brought out by the use of this analytical scheme. There is wide variation in the extent to which emotional feelings or emotional displays are the more important elements in the local repertoire of emotions. Historical studies (Stearns and Stearns, 1988) have shown that bodily feelings (sensations) had little role in the conception of emotions current among English speakers in the seventeenth century, while there is also good reason to believe that it is feelings above all that dominate the emotion culture of pre-European Polynesia with a precise taxonomy of the states of the internal organs (Harré, 1981).

Emotionologies

Words used for describing emotional feelings and displays are rarely used to express emotions. If someone says, "I'm envious of you," it is almost sure that the judgment they are thus expressing is not a display of that envy that figures among the seven deadly sins. What then is the relation between the vocabulary and the display? In research into emotion systems, we can study the way people use their emotion vocabulary, in commenting upon, describing, and reprimanding people for emotional displays and feelings. But we can also study emotion displays and feelings as discursive acts in themselves. We will follow Stearns and Stearns (1988) in calling the former the study of an "emotionology." An emotionology includes the ways the people in a particular local culture identify, classify, and recognize emotions. To study an emotionology, one must try to discover the rules of use of the local vocabulary of emotion words.

The study of the uses of the vocabulary of emotion words used by a certain group of people (it may be as small as a family and as large as a nation) allows us to abstract a "theory of emotion" that obtains in a particular culture at a particular time. Such a theory will rarely be stated explicitly but is immanent in the ways that words are used in describing and commenting upon the ways that emotions are displayed and felt. Sometimes, as in our era, the official "theory of the emotions," as it was offered by academic psychologists prior to the development of emotion studies from the discursive point of view, can be very far from expressing the theory implicit in the emotionology of the culture.

To analyze an emotion vocabulary to abstract the local theory of emotion, we must direct our studies to making explicit the rules and conventions for the use of the expressions of that vocabulary, such as "chagrined," "grief-stricken," "elated," "over-the-moon," even "sick-as-a-parrott"!

The "rules" for the correct use of an emotion word fall naturally into four groups.

The four sets of rules reflect four different features of the feeling or display of an emotion that we pay attention to when identifying it. We shall illustrate this scheme with a rough characterization of the use of the word *elated*.

1. The first relevant feature is a felt bodily disturbance. Many emotions, though not all, involve felt bodily disturbances. When does one use the word *elated*? There is a certain diffuse bodily feeling the biochemical basis of which a neurophysiologist might research into.

2. The second relevant feature is a characteristic display. There are several ways of displaying what *we* would call "elation." Laughing, smiling, or even crying and/or dancing about are all possible in our culture. The members of another culture or some moiety of ours (say, the members of the Marylebone Cricket Club at Lords) would not display elation in the way a soccer player might. Ekman and Oster (1979) have used the expression "display rules" for the cultural conventions that determine how an emotion should be expressed. These conventions will be reflected in the rules for the use of the term *elation* by each group of speakers.

3. The third relevant feature that is involved in the choice of an emotion word is the judgment that the feeling, disturbance, or display expresses. To simplify the matter for purposes of exposition, we could say that a display of elation expresses the judgment that something specially good has happened for which one has some responsibility.

4. The fourth relevant feature is the social act that the display performs or, as Austin called it, the "illocutionary force" of what is said or done. In the case of the rules for the use of the word *elation*, the display will be correctly called "elation" if it can be seen to have the force of a self-congratulation yet is neither vainglorious nor falsely modest.

We shall assume that these four conditions exhaust the rules for the use of emotion words. Are they also the components of the emotion? It will turn out to be much more complicated than that. One can't just say that the obtaining of these four conditions constitutes the having or being of an emotion. Emotions are brought into being in the interaction between actual or imagined persons in well-structured episodes and in specific historical conditions. At this stage of the analysis, all we can reasonably say is that these sets of rules reflect the conditions for calling someone "angry."

Sometimes, it turns out, for some emotions and for some occasions, some constituent of the above four-component comprehensive scheme does not have a part to play in the rules for the use of a word. When do we use the word *proud* (of someone)? Sometimes we say that someone is proud when we want to draw attention to a persistent attitude that is manifested in their way of treating other people. Only conditions 2, 3, and 4 above are met. Used in this way, *proud* does not seem to be an emotion word at all. Yet we also have the usage "feeling proud of . . ." Here there is perhaps a diffuse bodily feeling, but once again the weight is on conditions 2, 3, and 4. What is expressed is an opinion or judgment, but unlike the judgments expressed in, say, displays of fear, this judgment does have premises, in the sense that it would be astonishing if someone who was displaying pride could not give any reasons for so doing.

Emotion Words and Moral Implications of Displays

The physiological theory of emotion suffers from a serious weakness, evident in all the examples so far discussed. The felt physiological state is diffuse and indeterminate while the display of the emotion is precise and sharply distinguished. The third and fourth aspects of the conditions for the uses of emotion words, those that pick out the discursive side of the emotions, come to be dominant. We can illustrate the cognitive complexity of emotion displays and feelings by a brief summary of the emotionology of *envy* and *jealousy*. But why was envy taken to be one of the seven deadly sins?

What was so bad about envy? In contemporary English the word *envy* and cognate expressions are used for two rather different emotions. We shall refer to the sinful emotion as *malign envy,* and the morally innocuous emotion as *benign envy.* To differentiate the rules for the two uses of *envy*, let us imagine a situation in which A possesses some highly desirable good; B does not but would like to. Knowing that A has this desirable object X, B displays envy (is envious). Suppose the good is an academic honor, say, a desirable fellowship. Which of the two main kinds of envy would we say B displayed?

Malign and benign envy are not distinguishable at this level of analysis. We have to go into the kinds of relationships, defined in the local moral order, in which B stands to A and X. There are two broad possibilities as to how B could think that A's possession of X affects him or her.

1. Malign envy: B takes A's possession of X to be demeaning to him- or herself.
2. Benign envy: B would dearly like X but is neutral or pleased for A to have it and does not judge him- or herself demeaned by A's possession of the good.

The difference between B's emotion shows clearly in what one might call B's subsequent "strategy." Suppose A is a colleague of B in the same "team," or member of the same family, and B feels some reflected glory. B warmly and sincerely congratulates A while being benignly envious.

In the case of malign envy, B's congratulations are hollow, and this may appear in his or her expression. B's strategies are very different than those of the benignly envious. B can belittle X ("Fellowships like that don't mean very much!") or B can belittle A ("He doesn't really deserve that grant—the results he got were more by good luck than skill!"). B might even, in certain circumstances, attempt to deprive A of X or even destroy X.

In setting out these observations, we are working out further features of the system of rules that express the norms of some of the correct uses for the word *envy*. It should be clear, now, why people thought malign envy was one of the seven deadly sins. It expresses an evil attitude on the part of the envious person to the person of whom they are envious.

The analysis so far has revealed certain general conventions or rules that express the meaning-as-use of the words *envy* and *jealousy*. For an understanding of particular cases, more details would be needed. For instance, while one can indeed be benignly envious of someone receiving a well-deserved honor, one may be quite unmoved by seeing someone toting a Dunhill briefcase! This points to the need for a detailed ethnography to be included in any working psychology of the emotions, particularly when we try to explain the emotional lives of particular people. We need to take account of *local* values and *local* moral orders.

Historical Changes in the Referents of Emotion Words

Stearns and Stearns (1988) have looked at the changing meaning of the word *anger* among English speakers over the last 300 years. In the emotionology of the English speakers of Massachusetts and of England itself in the seventeenth century, the medium through which both judgment and act were assumed to be conveyed was the public display. Private feelings were not taken to be referents of this and other common emotion words. What was meant by saying that someone was angry was not that they were experiencing a certain bodily feeling but that they were expressing their outrage and engaging in reprimand by putting on a certain display. What feelings went along with that display were irrelevant to the use of the emotion word. This is not a behaviorism of the emotions because the display is not just a (conditioned or natural) response to stimuli but the expression of a judgment of what someone else has done.

By studying diaries, plays, and other documents, historians have followed the way the use of certain key emotion words changed over the following 100 years. The history of the uses of the word *anger* is quite typical. The change is striking. Words that were used almost exclusively for behavior, for conduct, and almost never for bodily feelings, in the beginning of the eighteenth century have, by the middle of the nineteenth century, expanded their domain to include bodily feelings as well. In the course of roughly the same period, the word *emotion* itself changed its meaning. From a word for the agitated behavior of a crowd as one might see it from an elevated position—that is, people running around—it came to mean extravagant individual behavior of an emotional kind. By the end of the eighteenth century, it had started to take over some of the work of the old concept of sentiment in that it began to be used to refer to bodily feelings. By the mid-nineteenth century, bodily feelings were becoming dominant in the meaning not only of the word *emotion* itself but also in many of the words in the common emotion lexicon.

Something else was happening. The gender of emotions was shifting in the English-speaking world, from being feelings and displays freely available to both men and women, to being the special preserve of women. In the nineteenth century, emotions became feminized and sentimentalized. Men had very rudimentary emotions or none at all. Of course, we have no idea what anyone was feeling in a family fracas in 1860, but we do know the rules of use for the words they would have used to describe it. It is important to see that our contemporary way of understanding emotion words as referring both to feelings and to displays, at least in the English-speaking world, is a recent development. From the discursive point of view, we have moved to a new cultural nexus in which we are able to interpret those feelings as the expression of the relevant judgments and as having the relevant illocutionary force.

Emotion Displays as Discursive Acts

If emotion feelings and displays are to be understood as embodied judgments on matters of morality, aesthetics, and prudence, they must occupy their proper places in unfolding episodes, to be analyzed something like conversations. In this way we can study the kinds of judgments that displays of emotions express and the kinds of acts they accomplish. According to the discursive theory, in those cultures in which both feelings and displays are taken to be properly described in terms drawn from the emotion vocabulary, there should be both private and public expression of embodied judgments and of the relevant social acts. They will be private when feelings are the bodily medium, and public when the medium is display. But it has not always been so, as we have seen in the research of historians of emotionologies. Nor is this tidy parallel between the private and the public realms to be found in all contemporary cultures.

The circumstances that bring forth a display that is properly to be called "anger" are effective only insofar as the angry person takes the other to have done what they did intentionally and without right. In a sense, these are not circumstances at all but the initial acts in a sequence of acts, assignable to discursive categories and held together by conventions and rules.

In studying the discursive role of expressions of emotion in contemporary English-speaking society, we must take account of both media of expression, namely, feelings and displays. Let us begin with some observations about the semiotics of emotional displays. According to the discursive theory, emotion displays have a double discursive function. The feeling you have, the display you put on, expresses an evaluative judgment, which may be one of three kinds.

1. There are moral judgments, such as displays of anger that express the judgment that the action of another person is a transgression of some sort against he or she who is seen or heard to be angry, or the judgments as to moral rights that are expressed in feelings and displays of envy and jealousy.

2. There are aesthetic judgments. Adverse aesthetic judgments have not been much favored as a topic by students of the aesthetic emotions. What adverse aesthetic judgments are conveyed by a

display of disgust? A recent study, done at Georgetown University by a student (Hal Isaacs) as an undergraduate research topic, showed that, for young middle-class Americans, disgust is highly tactile. A display of disgust expressed the judgment that something either actually felt, or would if touched feel, nasty. There were refinements, of course, and considerable individual variation on what "nastiness" counted as disgusting.

3. There are prudential judgments. A feeling of fear, a generic bodily state so interpreted, serves to express a premiseless prudential judgment that whatever we take as its object (that which brought about the feeling, perhaps causally, of course) is dangerous. Displaying fear can warn others that there is something deemed to be dangerous, and thus the display comes to have the force of an illocutionary act, a warning.

Emotion displays are not just physiologically caused bodily reactions to stimuli. They are meaningful displays, performed according to local conventions. Sarbin (1987) has pointed out that, if we look at the means by which the illocutionary force or social act meaning of emotion displays is manifested, we notice the very large role of convention. According to Sarbin, in expressing illocutionary force, that is, in performing the social act, as an emotion display, we adhere to certain dramatistic conventions. For example, when someone is displaying grief, the illocutionary force is quite complicated, but it includes the expression of regret. The judgment component might be that one has suffered a serious loss. This is somewhat oversimplified but is enough for illustrative purposes. Sarbin's question can be put this way: How does one do "grief"? The loss does not cause the feeling or the correlated display. If that is right, there must be intention involved and there must be right and wrong ways of performing an emotion display. According to Sarbin, the expressions of illocutionary force, of social acts, as displays are subject to local standards of correctness, which he suggests one should call "dramatistic conventions."

At English funerals, everybody presents a quite serious demeanor but only one or two people are expected actually to weep, usually the close female relatives. The discourse is in subdued tones. Even when one attends a funeral where one suspects that the widow would really rather like to dance on the grave of her late husband, still the dramatistic conventions are observed. In the countries of the Eastern Mediterranean, for instance, in Greece and in Israel, funeral conventions are rather different. The displays of grief are very dramatic. We have been told that in remote country areas of Greece there are still women who specialize in extravagant (by our standards) funeral displays, professionally. The force and sincerity of the mourners' performance can be assessed and understood only relative to the local dramatistic conventions. It would be quite wrong to say that the people of the Levant are grieving more deeply or sincerely than are Western Europeans. The difference in the force of the displays reflects differences in the conventions by which the required illocutionary force is expressed. And that may be the same in both regions. To make use of a familiar distinction in social psychology and ethology, the actions may be different but the acts they express may be the same.

Emotions and the People Who May Display Them

A useful schema for analyzing episodes from a discursive point of view is the "positioning triad" (Hollway, 1984). There is a mutual determination of three elements in a discourse: the story line evolving in an episode, the relative positions of speakers with respect to the local conventions of rights and duties of speaking or otherwise displaying judgments and/or expressing illocutionary acts, and the social acts they perform. Not everyone has the right or the duty to perform every emotion on every occasion. Just what act a person displaying some emotion is performing is relative to the story line that is taken to be immanent in the episode. The "positioning triad" helps us to analyze the dynamics of real evolving situations in order to track down the roles of the people engaging in these emotion displays. In the example we have just cited, the words *grief* (English) and *eillas* (modern Greek) are, more or less, mutually translatable. The "positioning triad," with which we would analyze the performances of those present, should yield a common structure in both, though the dramatistic conventions differ widely. The practices to which the Greek and English words are relevant are somewhat different in tone and in force but we might say that these words refer to species of the same genus.

Exotic Emotions, Their Modes of Display, and the Positioning Triads in Which They Occur

However, there are emotionologies and emotion display systems that are not mutually translatable in a one-to-one correspondence of terms with any of our Indo-European vocabulary or our customary "Western" emotion repertoire. How could this possibly be known? The way in which the similarities and differences between the emotions of an exotic culture and our own system was unraveled we owe largely to the work of Catherine Lutz.

The work with which Lutz (1988) brought to light the emotionology and emotional practices of the Ifaluk was, as far as possible in a piece of empirical work subject to the exigencies of life on a coral atoll, a practical application of the theories we have been expounding. She began with a study of the emotionology of the Ifaluk people, that is, of the diversity of their "emotion" terms and the rules of use of their vocabulary for talking about those matters that were roughly comprehended under what we call "emotions." She also looked at the situations and events and episodes that people described by using these words. In this way she tackled both sides of the "emotion" research question as we see it. She carefully and in detail described the local emotionology, by attention to the relevant vocabulary. Then, using her knowledge of this emotionology, she found out how emotion displays, as embodied judgments and social acts, were integrated into the episodes of everyday life on Ifaluk.

There was no word in the emotion vocabulary of the Ifaluk that could be translated directly into an English equivalent. There

were, however, some parallels and some similarities of usage. With
the help of clusters of English words, Lutz was able to construct a
preliminary emotionology for the Ifaluk language. She developed
this into a full-fledged system by using her rough scheme in con-
junction with numerous anecdotes, tales, and reports to link up
Ifaluk words into functionally significant clusters.

Ifaluk emotionology is very action oriented, somewhat similar
in general tone to that described by Stearns and Stearns (1988) as
realized in the uses of the emotion vocabulary of the seventeenth-
century English. Let us now illustrate these points with an example
from Lutz's emotionology for Ifaluk.

Metagu is a word that has a usage something akin to our words
fear, anxiety, and *embarrassment.* But one must delete from one's
interpretation of this word the specific reference to bodily feeling
characteristic of modern English usage of these terms. The function of the display is the central issue. The structure of the Ifaluk
emotionology is based on the principle that the emotions are all
essentially relational. A is seen to do *ker,* an emotion displayed in
a kind of excited behavior. It may be because he has caught a very
large fish. But this display is inappropriate for someone of A's
social standing in the presence of an important person, B. B displays *sort,* that is, roughly something like justified indignation at
the presumption of A in doing *ker* in his presence. On being confronted by B's display of *sort,* A displays *metagu.* If B sees A's
display as metagu, the episode is over. Here we have a discursive
cycle in which a display of metagu has its proper place.

What emotion is *metagu*? According to the thesis of the discursive theory of the emotions, to answer that question, we have to
ask what judgments are expressed in this cycle, and what illocutionary acts performed? To display "ker" is to proclaim something
like this: "Aren't I a splendid fisherman?" with the illocutionary
force of saying, for example, "I'm great." But one of A's standing
must be humble in the presence of B. B's display of "sort" expresses
the judgment, "You are a brash fellow," and has the illocutionary
force of a reprimand. A's display of "metagu" completes the cycle
by expressing a self-deprecatory judgment, "I behaved inappropri-

ately," with the illocutionary force of an apology. The cycle once completed restores the social fabric, in much the way that displays of embarrassment do in our emotion system.

But this rough gloss needs further elaboration. What happens in moments of physical danger? In those conditions the proper emotion is *rus*. From our point of view, we would expect it to be a species of some generic "fear" emotion of which "metagu" was also a species. But this is not so among the Ifaluk. In their emotionology, *rus* is a species of a genus of emotions of which "panic" is a prominent species. There is even a touch of "despair" or "hopelessness." More interesting though than the judgment "The situation is beyond me, I know not what to do!" is the illocutionary force of a display of "rus." It is a disclaimer of responsibility for the dangerous situation.

In examining the way the Ifaluk construe and use their vocabulary, we are touching on an emotionology that has a unique structure, different than any of the many versions of ours. It is a system of interrelated concepts, which can be made intelligible to us by paying attention to the way people are positioned in their social encounters. Lutz (1988) has not imported much of our emotion vocabulary and emotionology across cultural boundaries in giving us her interpretation. The common human themes through which the world of Ifaluk is made intelligible to us are such matters as social differentiation, honor, and dignity.

Emotion Displays and Their Verbal Equivalents

Our analyses in particular cases can be tested by finding speech-acts that would be functionally equivalent in the given context to the displays and feelings through which our moral, aesthetic, and prudential judgments and our performative acts are expressed. One could *say*, "You have offended against my rights. I wish to protest at your behavior and I reprimand you for it!" Or one could say, "I realize that I have just broken a social convention. However, I do know the rules. I am sorry for my offense." Why then do we

have fist shaking, shouting, and so on, and squirmings and em-
barrassed blushings? We suggest that an emotional display has a
great deal more force, in most circumstances, than does the verbal
expression of the very same judgment, however emphatically
it may be delivered. But the reason may lie somewhat deeper.
Wittgenstein offered some very powerful arguments in support of
the idea that there could not be rule-bound, normatively controlled actions if there were not natural regularities serving, so to
speak, as the generic models for every specific cultural practice.
He was also at pains to point out that the conditions that made
rule-following possible did not license a reduction of intentional
and meaningful action to the effects of causes. It seems reasonable
to say that we have systems of norms of conduct because we are
acquainted with certain natural regularities in our responses to
certain rather crudely defined situations, personal and physical. It
is these that serve as the conditions for the possibility of the diverse
and refined emotion systems and their accompanying emotionologies that we find when we look about us at how real people go on
in real life, whether in Oxford or on Ifaluk.

Conclusion

Emotions cannot be understood merely as physiological reactions to stimuli. Emotion displays and emotion feelings have a
cognitive role as bodily expressions of premiseless judgments
about stimulus situations. By studying the vocabularies through
which emotions are described and catalogued in particular cultures, we find that there are both bodily and cognitive criteria for
the use of emotion words. There are certain characteristic feelings
and displays and there are certain judgments expressed and social
acts performed in those feelings and displays. Each vocabulary
expresses a local taxonomy and theory of the emotions, an "emotionology." By testing for the meaningfulness of verbal equivalents
to emotion displays and feelings, it is possible to investigate the
significance of these displays and feelings in evolving episodes.

Three different topics seem to be addressed in these expressions: moral (e.g., "jealousy"), aesthetic (e.g., "delight"), and prudential (e.g., "dread"). We must see emotion displays and feelings as discursive acts, based upon both natural and inculcated patterns of bodily reaction but with meanings defined by their role in the discursive interactions of members of particular cultures.

❖ 10 ❖

Perception and Consciousness

What is consciousness? This question has dogged scientific psychology because it has about it the aura of a mystery. It seems more tractable, however, when approached via a study of perception. The Cartesian theory of perception has provided the inspiration for most contemporary psychological approaches and therefore it is that model to which we must turn before we attempt to reformulate the problems associated with these two varieties of subjectivity.

Perception

According to Descartes (1641), "There is indeed in me a certain passive faculty of sensing or receiving and cognizing ideas of sensible things." He believed that these ideas were produced in us by the action of external bodies on our sensory faculties. Our knowing of those things was based on the internal or mental states that both were produced by and resembled those bodies. This was the origin of the doctrine of internal representations, which has held sway in philosophy and psychology for so long that it is almost part of "common sense." Locke and the British empiricists took over the doctrine virtually unchanged from Descartes's formulation; "Fire may burn our Bodies, with no other effect, than it does a Billet, unless the motion be continued to the brain, and there the sense of Heat, or Idea of pain, be produced in the Mind, wherein consists actual Perception" (Locke, 1975 [1689]). Locke and Hume, and to a considerable extent the later empiricists, all assumed an atomistic theory of perception in which simple sensory components were assembled, by reason of their co-occurrence in experience, into complex wholes in which objects and significant patterns could be discerned.

Perception, when conceived of in this way, can be studied as scientifically as one likes. A typical paradigm would be that of psychophysics in which one delivers documentable intensities and configurations of stimulation and asks the subjects to report what they perceive. The paradox that these stimuli are only ideas in the mind of the experimenter was left to Berkeley to develop. This is a paradigm that may work well for circumscribed modes of stimulation, but more sophistication is needed to come to grips with the way in which the mind deals with more complex influences from the perceptual world in which people find themselves. To move from atomistic bits of sensory input to a holistic but differentiated perception of the world required a massive task of construction to be performed by the perceiver. In consequence, this view focused the attention of psychologists on trying to invent a picture (model) of a quasi-rational Cartesian mechanism that might perform the constructional task.

The first consideration that concerned workers, such as Helmholtz (1986), in the early days of perceptual psychology, was to discern how individuals might come, through perception, to a knowledge of the world around them. Helmholtz expressed the central problem as that of accounting for the fact that visual percepts have the property that "such objects are always imagined as being present in the field of vision as would have to be there in order to produce the same impression on the nervous mechanism, the eyes being used under ordinary normal conditions" (Helmholtz, 1866). His explanation was that of Locke, Hume, and the empiricists.

The Gestalt psychologists, such as Kohler, were not convinced. They argued that the pervasiveness of certain features of perception, such as the grouping of stimuli and the discernment of objects, could only be explained in terms of organization imposed on the sensory array. Thus their understanding of perception was as follows: "pattern of stimulation—organization—response to the products of organization" (Kohler, 1929). Their concerns remain central to the setting up of a properly scientific psychology. Among those concerns we should always bear in mind the problem of accounting for the fact that the act of perception constitutes wholes as recognizable objects or notable features of the environment. We should also bear in mind the closely allied fact that perception involves the identifying of figure as distinct from ground in each percept or tract of experience in the world. The Gestalt school in general tended to explain these principles of organization by means of innate cerebral mechanisms but their observations do not require this hypothesis and we will try to account for them in other ways.

The idea that the mind brings ordering principles to experience is, as we have noted, an important part of the tradition that followed Immanuel Kant (1929 [1789]). He made no claims himself about the origin of the ordering principles, asserting that this was an empirical question. He maintained that they were, for the purposes of his analysis, necessary conditions for the origin of knowledge from experience in general. He argued for an intrinsic connection between perception and knowledge, the implication being that the essential task of psychology was to show how sensory matter came to be combined with concepts in an orderly way so as to yield knowledge of the environment. Kant's essential insight, concerning the role of concepts in our experience of the world and ourselves, will emerge as one of the keys to our investigation of subjectivity.

His concern raises the entire question of the interrelationship between cognition and perception. Somehow we must derive from the contact our senses afford us with the environment an understanding of what that environment contains. Is this a matter of *inference* as theorists such as Gregory (1970) and philosophers such as Ayer (1973) claim, or is it something more basic and direct? Theorists who espouse the inference-to-a-conception-of-the-world view of perception have tried to chart the structure of the inferential patterns involved beginning with the data as presented to the eye of the subject. Their approach is clearly derived from the idea that the mind is an internal or Cartesian data-cruncher generating some surveyable facsimile or representation of the world as it is objectively known to be according to the natural sciences. If the world is represented by "ideas" and those are what we know, by what inner eye do we discern them? Even if this paradox is somehow bypassed, the task is, of course, fiendishly difficult. What is more, its terms do not square with the phenomenology of perception; for instance:

> The appearance of objects changes constantly as we move through the environment, but this rarely produces any apparent difficulty in identifying objects or in making sense of our environment. (Eysenck and Keane, 1990, p. 35)

Also, we know that some of the most basic stimuli for a child are such things as the human face, the direction of gaze of proximate adults (Butterworth, 1991), and yet, in physical terms, these are desperately complex geometrical configurations to derive from the available visual stimuli conceived as physically specifiable atoms. Therefore we need some way of understanding perception that accounts for the primacy of such stimuli as these. We need an account that allows us to adapt to the world in which we live and not the posited representational world that is supposed to "live" in us (i.e., that has "ecological validity"; Neisser, 1976) and yet that takes seriously the fact that concepts and conceptions of objects are intimately involved in perception and experience. Above all, we need an account of perception that does not postulate some inner eye (or "homunculus") that scans the "internal" representation of the world that we have obtained through the channels of the outer eye (Kenny, 1992).

One attempt to meet the first two of these desiderata was Gibson's (1979) theory of direct perception. Gibson believed that the problematic character of perceptual psychology came from adherence to the constructivist/inferential account of perceptual experience and its associated research program. He argued that perception was direct and involved picking up the characteristics of the optic array and using those directly to influence our responses to the world.

His program is well suited to account for the adaptation of perceptual systems to the world in which they find themselves. It avoids the positing of increasingly complex formally described representations of the world that enable computational transitions underpinning the organization of behavior. But there are real difficulties with his view, if it is presented as a comprehensive account of every facet of our perceptual skills.

The difficulties with taking the direct view of perception as a comprehensive theory are best outlined by considering the intentionality of perception. Perception is intentional in that the things we see have a certain meaning or significance for us. This intentional aspect of perception means that we do not merely perceive the extensional or objective array. When one perceives some feature of the world, one perceives it as being a certain way. A number of philosophers have discussed this as the mode of presentation of an object to a perceiver (Gillett, 1992a) or as "aspect seeing" (Wittgenstein, 1953). One may therefore be mistaken about an object, because the object-as-perceived is not the object-as-it-is. I might, for instance, see the "shadow" as my cat Blackie when in fact it is the neighbors' vicious pit bull terrier. Human beings are

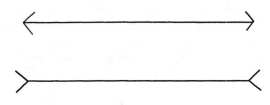

Figure 10.1. The Mueller-Lyer Illusion

also prone to typical illusions such as the Mueller-Lyer (Figure 10.1).

In Figure 10.1 we see as unequal two lines that are physically equal and we see them inaccurately because of supplementary "information" in the array. Thus it cannot merely be the physical characteristics of the array that shapes our experience but some synthesis based on the totality of the "information" we receive in the light of what we expect to perceive in such an environment. Indeed, perception seems to be generally informed by top-down categorizations, just as the Gestalt theorists were at pains to point out. We disambiguate unclear elements in the perceptual field by using context. We complete figures in the light of the wholes we take them to be and so on. Perceptions (or apparent perceptions) can even involve seeing objects that are not there such as the "person" who moves rapidly out of sight at the edge of one's vision in a dark house at night. Thus we need to posit some way in which the meaning or significance (intentionality) of the perception can be an intrinsic feature of our experience and not something added on to a direct response to the physical characteristics of the optical array.

Perhaps the most informative attempt to do this has been Ulrich Neisser's theory of the perceptual cycle.

Perception is indeed a constructive process, but what is constructed is not a mental image appearing in consciousness where it is admired by an inner man. At each moment the perceiver is constructing anticipations of certain kinds of information, that enable him to accept it as it becomes available. Often he must actively explore the optic array to make it available, by moving his eyes or his head or his body. These explorations are directed by the anticipatory schema which are plans for perceptual action as well as readinesses for particular kinds of optical structure. (Neisser, 1976, pp. 20-21)

Neisser appreciates the essential embeddedness of perception in the activity that it informs but he does not really advance beyond tentative suggestions about the roles of meaning and social context in this process. His account, though highly valuable as a way of refining Gibson's (1979) original theory without losing its main insights, is restrictively individualistic in the absence of further work in this area and we must look elsewhere to derive a more complete approach for our present purposes.

To those who expect a sociological turn at this point, the next theorist will be a surprise. Luria, whose work we have already cited with admiration, was a neuropsychologist deeply influenced by Vygotsky and the Russian tradition of activity psychology. He, like Neisser, is clear that perception is an active process that involves a dynamic interaction between the perceiver and world.

Perception . . . is an active process which includes the search for the most important elements of information, their comparison with each other, the creation of a hypothesis concerning the meaning of the information as a whole, and the verification of this hypothesis by comparing it with the original features of the object perceived. (Luria, 1973, p. 240)

Here we have all the features of the phenomenology rolled up in one conceptual bundle. But, over and above this synthetic contribution, Luria leaves us in no doubt as to the social character of the processes he is discussing.

He begins by noting the role of speech in perception as evidenced by a particularly elegant experiment. In a certain experimental situation, a child, as psychological subject, had to make a stereotyped movement in response to a pale pink stimulus but was not to make the movement when shown a darker shade of pink.

Luria elicited a successful response from the child in about half the trials and at a certain level of required reaction speed. The child was enabled to perform much better, however, when she was instructed to verbally categorize the shade of pink as dark or light at the same time as responding to it. Luria (1973) concludes:

> The inclusion of the child's own speech enabled the differential features to be distinguished, made sensitivity more selective, and made the responses much more stable. (p. 264)

This finding suggests that there is a deep relation between the use of symbols or meaningful markers and the dynamic perceptual process discussed by Neisser. It is a development of the view that "pattern recognition . . . is concerned with assigning meaning to visual stimuli" (Eysenck and Keane, 1990, p. 73). We should also note other phenomena that suggest that perception is deeply informed by what is meaningful. First, there are the data (originally obtained from work on subliminal perception) that suggest that perceptual recognition is subject to "semantic priming" whereby previous exposure to a stimulus related in meaning enhances perceptual performance on various tasks. There are also data to suggest that there is a phenomenon called "perceptual defense" whereby the perceptual mechanisms are selectively biased against the detection of negatively evaluated stimuli. This is, of course, highly paradoxical. After all, how can one know that a percept is going to contain such material before one recognizes it sufficiently clearly so as to know that one should block its recognition (Howie, 1952)? These findings encourage the idea that discourse penetrates a fair way into the perceptual system. A program focusing on the perceptual effects of discourse and one's positionings in various discourses begins to look plausible, even compelling. Luria himself contends that

> voluntary attention is not biological in its origin but a *social* act, and that it can be interpreted as the introduction of factors which are the product, not of the biological maturing of the organism but of forms

of activity created in the child during his relations with adults, into the complex regulation of this selective mental activity. (1973, p. 262)

His argument and conclusion are entirely congruent with the thrust of discursive psychology.

The discursive approach would understand perception as embedded in techniques and forms of life that provide one with certain skills of extracting information from the environment according to the conceptualizations that inform one's interactions with the world and others. Those skills are simultaneously enabling and constraining. They open up ways of adapting to and exploiting one's environment but they also become practiced and automatic such that the result of a given perceptual contact may, in the light of the anticipations it involves, become irresistible. Some of these perceptually "coercive" situations—such as seeing a moving object going past—are probably universal for human beings and reflect biological adaptations to features of the world. Others, and here one would particularly think of those that have to do with the important relationships and interactions in which we have a significant personal investment, draw their features from the settings in which the discursive skills of the perceiver has been shaped. Here one might think of noticing that a friend was absent from a gathering. The structure of subjectivity, in circumstances such as the latter, can only be explained on the basis of an understanding of the structure of the relevant discourse. Therefore—even if, in the former cases, a purely Gibsonian account will do very well— discursive aspects of a person's life are intrinsic to understanding their perceptual world. Of course, there is a sense in which this is always true but, for many commonplace encounters, the structure of discourse is so universally tied to relatively simple facts about human organisms and their operations on the environment that to call it discourse would be to broaden the term beyond its interesting and revolutionary use. This syncretic account is also to be found in Wittgenstein's treatment of perception (Wittgenstein, 1953, Pt. 2, sec. xi). The discursive act for him is the subsuming of the entity, as Gibson-perceived, under a type, the model being "seeing the likeness between two faces."

If we think of perception, in which features of the world seem to be "given" to us nonnegotiably, as reflecting necessary features of our discourse, then we can begin to understand both the prerational and the political nature of many of the fundamental psychological facts that contribute to the formation of human and social situations. Think, for instance, of the individual who has learned to perceive white people as smug, condescending, and exploitative. This person's mind is, perhaps, shaped by myriad situations in which just those properties were in evidence from whites both individually and collectively. The process may well have reached the point where certain gestures, expressions, and bodily stances when manifested in whites will be perceptually overlaid by meanings that are inseparable from the political overtones they have come to acquire. The fact that this is a perceptual fact means that it has an immediate impact on the way in which a situation is cognized, which is going to be difficult to change. It will have all the air of a "fact of nature." The possibilities of experience in the envisaged situation are so structured that the discourses meeting there preclude certain kinds of interpersonal understanding in the initial cycle of perception. Now, it is our contention that we cannot understand the structure of experience unless we take such discursive facts into account and give room, in psychological investigations, for those features to emerge. We must understand not only the situation as constructed by the investigator but also the significations available to the subject in order to unravel the nature of the perceptions constituting the topical moment in the subjectivity being studied.

Thus the understanding of perception as penetrated by discourse opens up for the investigator complexities that are somewhat daunting but also, one would hope, exciting, because they promise to bring us close to the real behavior of real people and the way in which those people derive information from their experiences in a dynamic and meaningful world. We must now turn to the fact that perceptions come as part of a greater whole that is a more or less integrated consciousness of the world and oneself in it.

Consciousness

Consciousness is a word derived from the Latin roots *con* and *scio*—"with" and "I know." This is an indication that, at least etymologically, the concept of consciousness involves interactive and discursive activity. But we need to investigate consciousness somewhat more closely to make good this tentative suggestion. We will do so by investigating its intentional structure.

The idea that consciousness and intentionality are essentially linked has a long philosophical history. Brentano regarded intentionality as the distinguishing characteristic of the mental (1929, p. 41) and went on to explore the phenomenology of our consciousness of objects and ourselves. He thought, as many philosophers do, that the defining characteristic of any mental event or state (if we can use those terms) is its intentional content or what it is about. Thus, for instance, if I think of myself as <noticing a snake beside the path> then the snake beside the path is essential to the identification and description of that mental occurrence. We can see this by positing the following situation. I noticed a snake beside the path and felt an involuntary shiver of fear. Thus what I am aware of in the situation could be said to include two different components or attributes; one is my noticing the snake and the other my shiver of fear. Now, what is it that makes there be two distinct features of what I am aware of here? They occur at the same time and in the same place and yet we consider them as separable. I might not have felt fearful or, less easy to imagine, I might not have consciously noticed the snake despite its causing my fear (in this case, I would have said something like "I feel fearful but I can't see anything to be fearful of"). Brentano's answer would be that they are distinct psychological or mental ascriptions because they have different *intentional objects*. In the one I am aware of a snake and in the other I am aware of my own fear. This may be all very sound philosophy but we still need to explain what all this has to do with consciousness.

Here we slip into discursive mode and begin with the experience of the ordinary person as illuminated by the discourses we use to capture our understanding of the concepts that cluster in this area. Hume noted that he could not catch himself as a mental being devoid of any experience, that is, as the being that does the experiencing or has the experiences. However hard he looked, he always found himself perceiving this or that, thinking of the other or focusing on some topic (Hume, 1969 [1740], p. 676). This is reflected in the language that surrounds the concept of consciousness. One is said to be "aware of the sleeping dog," "attending to the phrasing of the adagio"; one "has one's attention drawn to the use of light in the foreground," "is conscious of an air of tension in the room," and so on (Harré, 1983). In each case we are told not only of a state of an experience but of its object. Of course, we do speak of thinking of nothing in particular or being in a state of vacant enjoyment but in each of these cases we can usually say something about what the contents of consciousness are. It is just that they are not important or closely focused.

There are also locutions in which we say that someone is conscious (*simpliciter*), for instance, to mark the fact that they have recovered from the effects of a blow on the head. It is interesting that we establish that by asking about specific objects of consciousness. Thus, in assessing the time of recovery from concussion, one might ask the subject something like this: "What was the first thing you became *aware* of?" which is an intentional question if ever there was one.

This cluster of significations goes to determine what we call, in a broad and general way, "being conscious." Each of them is used to describe a situation in which a set of conditions gives rise to a meaningful orientation of the perceiver. In each case there is some significance or other attached by the person to what is presented. A person may not be sure just what significance to attach and therefore his or her conscious experience may be ambiguous but it will (essentially) have some content, however vague. Thus "I was conscious that something or someone was there but I cannot now and could not then say what it was." Here we would want to say that a person is in an intentional state but it is one that they cannot signify in any way that they feel confident about; that is, they cannot put it into a kind or category. If consciousness were an internal realm of self-declaring images whose identity was infallibly known to the conscious person (as Cartesian theorists have often taken it to be), this kind of report would be nonsensical. In fact, this kind of report, perhaps in slightly less vague forms, is a common part of the phenomenology of each of us. It fits rather neatly with the view that mental life involves the exercise of discourse-related skills that are applied in situations according to the subjectivity of the individual concerned.

Taken together, these considerations suggest that consciousness is best thought of as the capacity to focus cognitive abilities on a range of objects, events, and conditions around the subject. When I think of a thing, I think of it as being thus and so. It is an object for me and for you, but for me it may be a handle that will enable me to escape from the room and for you merely a protruding feature on the wall. On this account, consciousness is discursive and loaded with conceptual content that may be well or ill defined but that expresses the discursive orientation of the subject. Thus the content of conscious experience is given not only by what it is one is conscious of but also by the discursive skills I bring to bear on it. Thus, for instance, I can think of *that round object* but my consciousness has much more potential richness and usefulness if I think of it as being a globe of the world. In the first case, where I see it only as a round object, I may not be aware of many aspects of it but, in the second, there is a vast amount of further cognitive opportunity to my experience.

The capacity to bring a variety of conceptualizations or significations to bear on a situation is a mark of the mature and intellectually developed person, and, as we have noted, the degree of development and articulation of one's abilities in this area crucially depends on the quality and nature of the experiences and encounters that form the history of one's own subjectivity. Thus, for instance, children bound through the Louvre are conscious only of a limited amount of the content of the experiences to be had. When shown the Mona Lisa, some children recently remarked that they thought they had seen it before, and it was just an insignificant little brown picture with a whole crowd of people around it. The limits to their appreciation depended, of course, not on the quality of their sensory systems as physiological mechanisms or on the physical conditions in which their visit was conducted but on their individual histories of participation in the relevant *discourses*. As human beings extend their discursive skills (not merely the verbal expression of those skills), so they expand their consciousness; that is, they extend the range of matters to which they can attend and of which they are aware.

We can illustrate this with reference to the life experience of many who are diagnosed as having borderline personality disorder because of a history of petty violence, failed relationships, and aimless disorderly behavior (sometimes punctuated by dramatic episodes such as suicidal gestures or outbursts of sustained and spectacular aggression). When talking to such individuals, one finds that they are poor at articulating or understanding the events of their lives and the relationships among them. They tend to have a very limited discursive context within which to negotiate and elaborate their responses to life events. Their discourse is dominated by words and expressions (many of which are unprintable) like these: "I'll show them all," "putting people down," "getting back at them," "can't be bothered," "I don't know," "see if I care," and so on. All are limited. They indicate lack of insight and direction, particularly in interpersonal situations. This lack of depth and richness in the discursive content of their subjectivities translates itself into a human and relational lack in their lives in general.

The case of these unfortunate and limited subjects illustrates the fact that consciousness is the subjective springboard of agency. One cannot do that of which one cannot conceive and one cannot conceive of content for which one lacks the discourse-based skills. This is particularly true when the topic at the center of consciousness is oneself.

Self-Consciousness

The essential nature of self-consciousness emerges most clearly when we consider its relation to the awareness we have of and the attention we pay to things around us. Brentano (1929) explored self-consciousness in the course of trying to understand the structure of conscious experience:

> The thinking being, in thinking, always relates to more than one object; for example someone who sees, sees something coloured and at the same time perceives himself as the one who sees. (p. 41)

We might question whether "perceives" is the right word here but we cannot question the dual structure of consciousness such that I am conscious of a public object and also conscious of myself as being conscious of that thing (a secondary object). We have previously remarked the fact that a thought can be thought of as the application, in a certain set of conditions, of a concept (or discursive element) according to a rule. We pointed out that it was implicit in such an act (of applying a rule) that one was sensitive to the possibility of being right or wrong in one's use of the concept concerned. Now, the way in which one becomes sensitive to and competent in making judgments about the rightness or wrongness of a perception is by adapting to the judgments of others concerning one's use of the concept concerned. Thus, in learning to think, one learns to make discursive moves in what one takes to be the way that others make them and then to modify and adapt one's responses to conform to the practice of those others. Thus, in learning to use concepts—that is, learning to use the relevant words and other signs—I also, and essentially, learn to register the responses of others to me and what I do. However, if one can learn to imitate the discursive moves of others in relation to things around one (Brentano's primary objects), it seems quite plausible that one can also learn to imitate their responses to oneself as discursive subject (the secondary object). This is our account of the basis of self-consciousness (Harré, 1983, Chap. 6, sec. 4).

Notice that, if we extend our previous remarks about thought depending on the implicit norms shared by a discursively linked group, then my attitude to myself as thinker is a normatively colored object.

We can, however, add even further complexity to this appreciation of consciousness by drawing on the philosophy of Jean-Paul Sartre and noting the fact that one is also aware of oneself as an object of which others are aware (Sartre, 1958). Thus there is not only a framework of implicit norms that govern one's use of concepts and one's discursive acts, but a person also anticipates specific normative judgments about their behavior and character. This aspect of subjectivity introduces a special set of considerations into the kinds of thought and awareness that can inform a person and their experience. The normative framework builds implicit habits of reflection on the significations one uses in certain contexts but also encourages the self-reflexive adoption of the subjectivity of the other in one's framing of one's thoughts. Thus, for instance, a person might respond to a certain kind of violence as exhilarating but signify that as shock or horror. When faced with the fact that the allegedly horrid and negative experience is being sought out in preference to other possible contexts, the kind of conceptualization that is adduced to account for that fact will then reflect the attitudinal norms favored in a discourse within which someone locates themselves. One might, for instance, say that it has a fascination the person does not understand and that it is in some way morbid or connected with some inner mechanism. This tends to alienate the consciousness of the person seeking violence of that type from their central subjectivity or identity. In this way the normative structure of consciousness reflects both one's patterns of semantic usage but also, and inseparably, the evaluative features of the discursive contexts in which one finds oneself.

The realization that there is an evaluative structure intrinsic to consciousness and not merely a set of factual, representational, or knowledge-garnering activities allows us to further understand why formal theories of human cognition, based on mechanisms that do not have an interpersonal engagement in discourse, are misleading. A person does not and cannot become aware of certain things and think certain thoughts because to think those things would be to constitute a subjectivity that could not be their own. This gives us a special orientation toward the unconscious and its contents.

Freud's theory of the unconscious and the one taken up by later psychoanalytic and psychodynamic theories suggested that in the unconscious we tend to find primitive impulses that are frustrated from finding their natural expression. Thus we are told, for instance, in *Civilisation and Its Discontents* (Freud, 1985), that the social or communal human being is an unnatural, hybrid creature. On the one hand it is a person who has instincts and impulses that seeks satisfaction and on the other it is one who is subject to social forces that tends to repress, limit, and even distort those psychic dispositions into forms that create dissatisfaction and mental tension. In contrast to this approach, we have the existentialist view that the unconscious is a creation of bad faith, a fiction we have recourse to when we seek to separate from our core selves those aspects of self that do not fit our self-image.

A discursive conceptualization is distinct from both of these. It focuses on what can and cannot be said in a given context and notices the potential within a given complex subjectivity for there to be significations that cannot be manifested discursively (in a broad sense to include any form of symbolic display) in a given context of activity. Thus, for instance, if I am a "happily married and settled woman" who has "nothing to complain about" then it might be impossible for me to articulate to myself the fact that aspects of myself have been lost in this situation. The discourses in which I customarily move may only make available to me construals of my situation that suggest that it is adequate and fulfilling. Given that boundary to the sayable, I may not be able to find a ready signification for those aspects of my experience that I find inexpressible. My discursive resources are, of course, constituted and therefore limited by the conventions of the situations within which I live. Were I to be introduced into a different set of discourses, then I would find that my subjectivity became transformed because the vague feelings or intimations of absence were made explicit by becoming nameable. And here we can too readily slip into the trap of believing that the unnamed aspects of subjectivity were somehow ready-formed and articulated in an inner realm, the unconscious. These aspects of "me" are thought of as wanting only the indepth psychological skills of an analyst to bring them to the surface. Such a formulation subscribes to the idea of representation in which the world in general and my psyche in particular have contents that exist apart from any conscious activity of the persons who represent them. But discursive psychology sees this as a distortion based on the least contentious and most universal instances of signification whereby events and situations are invested with meaning. Those simple examples obscure the role of the subject.

For the most part, when I signify my mental life as involving, say, a neutralizing of my identity as an agent, something about me changes. The change makes it possible for that to be regarded as true or false in a way that it could not have been before and it results from my coming into relation with the discourse giving rise to that thought. My gaining access to that signification therefore alters my mental life. It does not merely provide a novel means for a redescription of it. What is more, the fact that there is a context in which I can articulate that signification changes the structure of my subjectivity.

In the present account, we focus not so much on the entities lurking in the Cartesian interior of a human subject (because there are none) but on the significations that are available and permitted within a given moral reality. This moral reality is a discourse, elucidated so that its power relationships, positionings, and effects on human beings are exposed. Consider, for instance, the setting in which a young man is located in a discourse involving the idea that commercial success can be combined with a ruthless disregard for the niceties of business ethics and care for the environment. Clients are talked of solely as objects for the purpose of profit making. In this discourse, one cannot ask questions as to what kind of human being one is becoming in adopting this discourse against a framework of certain moral significations such as commitment, mutuality, care, and so on. Those conceptualizations are not available to structure behavior or evaluate it within that discourse. Of course, they are not totally insulated from it because none of us ever inhabits such a narrow discursive context. The impingement of the multiple conceptual structures that are borne by the alternative discursive systems available in a society will create reflective tension within the subjectivity of one who stands at their intersection.

Conclusion

We therefore need to leave behind the idea that the structure of subjectivity is a multilayered psychic architecture in which self-contained psychological entities such as desires, beliefs, moral attitudes, intentions, character traits, and so on fight it out on the battleground of mental life. We need to see mental life as a dynamic activity, engaged in by people, who are located in a range of interacting discourses and at certain positions in those discourses and who, from the possibilities they make available, attempt to fashion relatively integrated and coherent subjectivities for themselves. This task or project is variably accessible to reflective scrutiny and thus carried on only in part at a level where cognitive/discursive resources can be focused and directed on it. The extent to which that can happen and the significations that are applied to the contexts in which people find themselves jointly determine the contents of consciousness and perception. These contents and their history are the core of an individual subjectivity.

❖ References ❖

Allport, D. A. 1983 "Language and cognition" in *Approaches to language* R. Harris (ed.) Oxford: Pergamon

Allport, G. 1937 *Personality: a psychological interpretation* London: Constable

Aristotle 1925 *Nichomachean ethics* (tr. D. Ross) Oxford: Oxford University Press

Averill, J. 1982 *Anger and aggression: an essay on emotion* New York: Springer-Verlag

Ayer, A. J. 1973 *The central questions of philosophy* Harmondsworth: Penguin

Baker, G. P. 1974 "Criteria, a new foundation for semantics" *Ratio XVI* 156-189

Bannister, D. & Mair, J. M. M. 1968 *The evaluation of personal constructs* London: Academic Press

Beach, F. A. 1965 "The snark was a boojum" in *Readings in animal behavior* T. E. McGill (ed.) New York: Holt Rinehart & Winston

Billig, M. (ed.) 1988 *Ideological dilemmas* London: Sage
Billig M. (ed.) 1991 *Ideology and opinions: studies in rhetorical psychology* London: Sage
Brentano, F. 1973 (1924) *Psychology from an empirical standpoint* London: Routledge & Kegan Paul
Brentano, F. 1929 *Sensory and noetic consciousness* (tr. M. Schattle & L. McAlister) O. Kraus (ed.) London: Routledge & Kegan Paul
Bruner, J. S. 1973 *Beyond the information given: studies in the psychology of knowing* New York: Norton
Bruner, J. S. 1990 *Acts of meaning* Cambridge, MA: Harvard University Press
Butterworth, G. 1991 "The ontogeny and phylogeny of joint visual attention" in *Natural theories of mind* A. Whiten (ed.) Oxford: Blackwell
Butterworth, G. 1993 "Theory of mind and the facts of embodiment" in *Origins of an understanding of mind* C. Lewis & P. Mitchell (eds.) Hove: Erlbaum
Cattell, R. B. 1966 *The scientific analysis of personality* Chicago: Aldine
Chomsky, N. 1972 *Language and mind* San Diego: Harcourt Brace Jovanovich
Davidson, D. 1980 *Essays on actions and events* Oxford: Clarendon
Davidson, D. 1984 *Inquiries into truth and interpretation* Oxford: Clarendon
Descartes, R. 1641 *Meditations on the first philosophy* (tr. J. R. Weinberg) New York: Adam & Tannery, Meditation 6
Ekman, P. & Oster, H. 1979 "Facial expression of emotion" *Annual Review of Psychology* 30 527-554
Eysenck, H. 1953 *The structure of human personality* New York: Plenum
Eysenck, H. & Eysenck, W. 1985 *Personality and individual differences* New York: Plenum
Eysenck, M. W. & Keane, M. T. (1990) *Cognitive psychology* Hove: Erlbaum
Fodor, J. 1968 *Psychological explanation* New York: Random House
Fodor, J. 1975 *The language of thought* New York: Crowell
Foucault, M. 1972 *The archaeology of knowledge* London: Tavistock
Frege, G. 1977 *Logical investigations* (tr. P. T. Geach & R. Stoothoff) Oxford: Blackwell
Freud, S. 1940 "An outline of psychoanalysis" *International Journal of Psychoanalysis* 21 27-84
Freud, S. 1985 "Civilisation and its discontents" in *Civilisation, society and religion* (Vol. 12) Harmondsworth: Penguin
Gibson, J. J. 1979 *The ecological approach to visual perception* Boston: Houghton Mifflin
Giddens, A. 1984 *The constitution of society* Cambridge: Polity
Gillett, G. 1992a *Representation, meaning and thought* Oxford: Oxford University Press

Gillett, G. 1992b "Language, social ecology and experience" *International Studies in the Philosophy of Science 5* 1-8

Gillett, G. 1993 "Humpty Dumpty and the night of the Triffids: individualism and rule following" *Synthese* 1993

Greenwood, J. D. 1992 "Discursive practices and psychological science" *American Behavioral Scientist 36* 114-123

Gregory, R. L. 1970 *The intelligent eye* New York: McGraw-Hill

Hacker, P. 1991 "Seeing, representing and describing: an examination of David Marr's computational theory of vision" in *Investigating psychology* J. Hyman (ed.) London: Routledge

Hacking, I. 1984 *Representing and intervening* Cambridge: Cambridge University Press

Harré, R. 1981 "Psychological variety" in *Indigenous psychologies* P. Heelas & A. Lock London: Academic Press

Harré, R. 1983 *Personal being: a rationale for the natural sciences* Oxford: Blackwell

Harré, R. (ed.) 1987a *The social construction of emotions* Oxford: Blackwell

Harré, R. 1987b "Persons and selves" in *Persons and personality* A. Peacocke & G. Gillett (eds.) Oxford: Blackwell

Harré, R. 1990 "Embarrassment: a conceptual analysis" in *Shyness and embarrassment* R. A. Crozier (ed.) Cambridge: Cambridge University Press, 181-204

Harré, R. & Secord, P. F. 1973 *The explanation of social behaviour* Oxford: Blackwell

Helmholtz, H. von 1925 (1866) *Physiological optics* (tr. J. P. C. Southall) New York: Optical Society of America

Hempel, C. G. 1965 *Aspects of scientific explanation* New York: Free Press

Henriques, J., et al. 1984 *Changing the subject* London: Methuen

Hollway, W. 1984 "Gender differences and the production of subjectivity" in *Changing the subject* J. Henriques et al. London: Methuen

Howie, D. 1952 "Perceptual defence" *Psychological Review 59* 308-315

Hume, D. 1969 (1740) *A treatise of human nature* E. C. Mossner (ed.) Harmondsworth: Penguin

Husserl, E. 1973 *Cartesian meditations* (tr. D. Cairns) The Hague: Nijhoff

Kant, I. 1929 (1789) *Critique of pure reason* (tr. N. Kemp Smith) London: Macmillan

Karmiloff-Smith, A. 1979 "A functional approach to child language" in *Cambridge studies in linguistics* Cambridge: Cambridge University Press

Karmiloff-Smith, A. 1986 "From metaprocess to conscious access: evidence from children's metalinguistic and repair data" *Cognition 23* 95-147

Kelly, G. A. 1955 *The psychology of personal constructs* New York: Norton

Kenny, A. 1991 "The homunculus fallacy" in *Investigating psychology* J. Hyman (ed.) London: Routledge

Kohler, W. 1929 *Gestalt Psychology* New York: Liveright

Lévi-Strauss, C. 1972 *The savage mind* London: Weidenfeld and Nicholson

Locke, J. 1975 (1689) *An essay concerning human understanding* P. Nidditch (ed.) Oxford: Clarendon

Luria, A. R. 1973 *The working brain* (tr. B. Haigh) Harmondsworth: Penguin

Lutz, C. 1988 *Unnatural emotions* Chicago: Chicago University Press

Lyman, S. M. and Scott, M. B. 1970 *A sociology of the absurd* New York: Appleton-Century-Crofts

Lyman, S. M. and Scott, M. B. 1975 *The drama of social reality* New York: Oxford University Press

Manicas, P. J. 1986 "Whither psychology?" in *Psychology: defining the discipline* J. Margolis et al. (ed.) Oxford: Blackwell

McArthur, L. Z. & Baron, R. M. 1983 "Toward an ecological theory of social perception" *Psychological Review* 90 215-238

McCarthy, R. A. & Warrington, E. K. 1990 *Cognitive neuropsychology* San Diego: Academic Press

McGill, T. E. (ed.) 1965 *Readings in animal behavior* New York: Holt, Rinehart & Winston

Mead, G. H. 1934 *Mind, self and society* Chicago: University of Chicago Press.

Miller, G. A., Galanter, E. & Pribram, K. 1967 *Plans and the structure of behavior* New York: Holt

Miller, G. A. & Johnson-Laird, P. N. 1976 *Language and perception* Cambridge: Cambridge University Press

Millikan, R. G. 1990 "Truth rules, hoverflies and the Kripke-Wittgenstein paradox" *The Philosophical Review* 94 323-353

Mischel, W. 1968 *Personality and assessment* New York: John Wiley

Muhlhausler, P. & Harré, R. 1991 *Pronouns and people* Oxford: Blackwell

Neisser, U. 1967 *Cognitive psychology* New York: Appleton-Century-Crofts

Neisser, U. 1976 *Cognition and reality* San Francisco: Freeman

Paivio, A. 1971 *Imagery and verbal process* New York: Holt, Rinehart & Winston

Parrott, W. G. 1993 "On the scientific study of angry organisms" in *Perspectives on anger and emotion: advances in social cognition* R. S. Wyer & T. Srull (eds.) Hillsdale, NJ: Erlbaum

Pearce, W. B. & Cronen, V. E. 1981 *Communication, action and meaning* New York: Praeger

Penfield, W. 1958 "Some mechanisms of consciousness discovered during electrical stimulation of the brain" *Proceedings of the National Academy of Sciences* 44 51-66

Pervin, L. 1970 *Personality, theory, assessment and research* New York: John Wiley

Pettit, P. 1990 "The reality of rule-following" *Mind* 99 1-22

Plato 1982 *Protagoras* (tr. B. A. F. Hubbard & E. S. Karnofsky) London: Duckworth

Potter, J. & Edwards, D. 1992 *Discursive psychology* London: Sage

Prince, M. 1978 (1905) *The dissociation of personality* Oxford: Oxford University Press

Pylyshyn, Z. 1979 "Imagery theory: not mysterious—just wrong" *Behavioral and Brain Sciences* 2 561-563

Pylyshyn, Z. 1984 *Computation and cognition* Cambridge, MA: MIT Press

Quinton, A. 1967 "The problem of perception" in *The philosophy of perception* G. J. Warnock (ed.) Oxford: Oxford University Press

Rosaldo, M. 1980 *Knowledge and passion: Ilongot notions of self and social life* Cambridge: Cambridge University Press

Ryckman, R. M. 1989 *Theories of personality* New York: Wadsworth

Sabat, S. R. & Harré, R. 1992 "The construction and deconstruction of self in Alzheimer's disease" *Ageing and Society* 12 443-461

Saffran, E. M. & Marin, O. S. M. 1975 "Immediate memory for word lists and sentences in a patient with deficient auditory short term memory" *Brain and Language* 2 420-433

Sajama, S. & Kamppinen, M. 1987 *A historical introduction to phenomenology* New York: Croom Helm

Sarbin, T. 1987 "Emotion and act: roles and rhetoric" in *The social construction of emotions* R. Harré (ed.) Oxford: Blackwell, Chapter 5

Sartre, J. P. 1958 *Being and nothingness* (tr. H. Barnes) London: Methuen

Schank, R. C. & Abelson, R. P. 1977 "Scripts, plans and knowledge" in *Thinking: readings in cognitive science* P. N. Johnson-Laird & P. C. Wason (eds.) New York: Cambridge University Press

Shweder, R. 1992 *Thinking through cultures* Cambridge, MA: Harvard University Press

Singer, J. L. & Kolligian, J. 1987 "Personality: developments in the study of private experience" *Annual Review of Psychology* 38 533-574

Sperry, R. 1965 "Brain dissection and the mechanisms of consciousness" in *The brain and conscious experience* J. Eccles (ed.) New York: Springer-Verlag

Stearns, C. Z. & Stearns, P. W. 1988 *Emotion and social change* New York: Holmes and Meier

Stich, S. P. 1983 *From folk psychology to cognitive science* Cambridge, MA: MIT Press

Strawson, P. F. 1959 *Individuals* London: Methuen

Taylor, C. 1964 *The explanation of behaviour* London: Routledge

Thorndike, E. L. 1913 *The psychology of learning* New York: Teachers College Press

Trevarthen, C. 1992 "The functions of emotions in early infant communication and development" in *New perspectives in early communication development* J. Nadel & L. Camioni (eds.) London: Routledge

von Cranach, M. & Harré, R. 1981 *The analysis of action* Cambridge: Cambridge University Press

Vygotsky, L. S. 1962 *Thought and language* Cambridge, MA: MIT Press

Vygotsky, L. S. 1978 *Mind in society* Cambridge, MA: Harvard University Press

Vygotsky, L. S. 1987 *Thinking and speech* New York: Plenum

Walter, W. G. 1968 "The contingent variation: an electrocortical sign of sensori-motor association in man" in *Brain Reflexes: Progress in Brain Research* 22 E. A. Astratyan (ed.) 364-377

Westcott, M. A. 1992 *The psychology of personal freedom* New York: Springer-Verlag

Wierzbicka, A. 1992 *Semantics, culture and cognition* New York: Oxford University Press

Winch, P. 1958 *The idea of a social science and its relation to philosophy* London: Routledge

Wittgenstein, L. 1953 *Philosophical investigations* (tr. G. E. M. Anscombe) Oxford: Blackwell

Wittgenstein, L. 1961 (1922) *Tractatus logico-philosophicus* (tr. D. F. Pears & B. F. McGuiness) London: Routledge & Kegan Paul

Wittgenstein, L. 1972 *Blue and brown books* Oxford: Blackwell

Wittgenstein, L. 1975 *Philosophical remarks* R. Rhees (ed.) Oxford: Blackwell

❖ Name Index ❖

❖ Subject Index ❖

❖ About the Authors ❖

Rom Harré is truly a Renaissance man. As lecturer, teacher, and philosopher, he has long been a preeminent and influential voice whose work is recognized in many disciplines. In the last 20 years he has been a pioneer in developing the theory and practice of discursive psychology. He is presently a Fellow of Linacre College, Oxford; Professor of Psychology at Georgetown University in Washington, DC; and Adjunct Professor of Philosophy at SUNY, Binghamton, NY. Author of more than 200 journal articles and 24 books, including *The Philosophies of Science, Second Edition* (1986), *Personal Being: A Theory for Individual Psychology* (1983), *Physical Being: A Theory for Corporeal Psychology* (1991), and *Social Being: Revised Edition* (1993). He has also edited or co-edited another 26 volumes, including the *Blackwell Encyclopedic Dictionary of*

191

Psychology (1985). He is the recipient of many academic awards including an honorary D.Pol. (Helsinki), an honorary D.Sc. (Brussels), and the Royden B. Davis Professor of Interdisciplinary Studies (1993). His interests range from the analyses of emotions to social theories and linguistics. A New Zealand native, Harré has held posts and lectured all over the world, most recently in China, the United States, Spain, the Netherlands, and Canada.

Grant R. Gillett has a unique combination of experience and interests as an internationally known neurosurgeon, philosopher, and teacher. He is currently a consultant neurosurgeon at Dunedin Hospital in New Zealand; Associate Professor in medical ethics, Bioethics Centre, University of Otago Medical School (where he established and developed the bioethics teaching course); and Honorary Lecturer in Philosophy, Otago University. In addition to teaching clinical neuroscience, philosophy, and psychology courses, Gillett serves as ethics adviser to the New Zealand Health Department and holds editorial board positions on eight journals, including the *Journal of Mind and Behavior, Social Science and Medicine,* and the *British Journal of the Philosophy of Science.* Widely published in the fields of philosophy, medical ethics, and philosophical psychology, he is also author of *Representation, Meaning and Thought* (1992), coauthor of *Practical Medical Ethics* (1992), and coeditor of *Medicine and Moral Reasoning* (1993). He is a Fellow of the Royal Australian College of Surgeons and a member of the New Zealand Neurological Association, Oxford Society for Applied Philosophy, and the Australian Association of Neurological Surgeons. He has also presented over 100 academic papers and addresses in Europe, the United States, Canada, and Australia.

LaVergne, TN USA
19 July 2010
190051LV00001B/48/A